# Mastering SQL For Interviews And Beyond

Anshuman Mishra

Published by Anshuman Mishra, 2025.

## MASTERING SQL FOR INTERVIEWS AND BEYOND

**INTRODUCTION:**
IN TODAY'S DATA-DRIVEN WORLD, SQL (STRUCTURED QUERY LANGUAGE) HAS BECOME AN ESSENTIAL SKILL FOR ASPIRING PROFESSIONALS IN THE SOFTWARE INDUSTRY. **"MASTERING SQL FOR INTERVIEWS AND BEYOND"** IS A COMPREHENSIVE GUIDE FOR ANYONE PREPARING FOR TECHNICAL INTERVIEWS AT LEADING SOFTWARE COMPANIES, AS WELL AS FOR COLLEGE STUDENTS AIMING TO EXCEL IN LAB-BASED SQL COURSEWORK. THIS BOOK IS THOUGHTFULLY DESIGNED TO EQUIP READERS WITH THE KNOWLEDGE, PROBLEM-SOLVING SKILLS, AND PRACTICAL EXPERTISE NEEDED TO SUCCEED IN REAL-WORLD SCENARIOS.

**WHY THIS BOOK?**
SQL IS NOT JUST A DATABASE LANGUAGE; IT IS A TOOL THAT EMPOWERS DEVELOPERS, ANALYSTS, AND DATA SCIENTISTS TO QUERY, MANIPULATE, AND MANAGE DATA EFFECTIVELY. INTERVIEWERS OFTEN TEST SQL KNOWLEDGE TO EVALUATE A CANDIDATE'S LOGICAL THINKING AND DATABASE HANDLING CAPABILITIES. **"MASTERING SQL FOR INTERVIEWS AND BEYOND"** BRIDGES THE GAP BETWEEN THEORETICAL KNOWLEDGE AND HANDS-ON PROBLEM-SOLVING, PREPARING READERS FOR SQL CHALLENGES IN INTERVIEWS AND PROFESSIONAL TASKS.

---

### KEY FEATURES:

1. **INTERVIEW-CENTRIC CONTENT:**
   - COVERS FREQUENTLY ASKED INTERVIEW QUESTIONS FROM TOP COMPANIES LIKE GOOGLE, AMAZON, MICROSOFT, AND MORE.
   - INCLUDES REAL-WORLD PROBLEM SETS WITH VARYING LEVELS OF DIFFICULTY.
   - FOCUSES ON QUERY OPTIMIZATION, JOINS, SUBQUERIES, AND ADVANCED SQL TECHNIQUES.
2. **STEP-BY-STEP SOLUTIONS:**
   - EACH PROBLEM IS EXPLAINED WITH A CLEAR, CONCISE, AND STEP-BY-STEP SOLUTION.
   - VISUAL AIDS LIKE QUERY DIAGRAMS AND RELATIONAL SCHEMA FOR BETTER UNDERSTANDING.

3. **PRACTICAL APPROACH:**
    - CASE STUDIES AND EXERCISES BASED ON REAL-WORLD SCENARIOS.
    - LAB-BASED EXPERIMENTS TO REINFORCE LEARNING.
    - TIPS FOR DEBUGGING AND WRITING EFFICIENT SQL QUERIES.
4. **STRUCTURED LEARNING:**
    - ORGANIZED INTO BEGINNER, INTERMEDIATE, AND ADVANCED SECTIONS.
    - CONCEPT CLARITY FOLLOWED BY HANDS-ON PRACTICE EXERCISES.
    - SAMPLE PROJECTS FOR DATABASE DESIGN AND IMPLEMENTATION.
5. **SPECIAL FOCUS AREAS:**
    - COMPLEX JOINS AND SET OPERATIONS.
    - WINDOW FUNCTIONS AND CTES (COMMON TABLE EXPRESSIONS).
    - TRANSACTIONS, INDEXING, AND DATABASE PERFORMANCE OPTIMIZATION.
    - ADVANCED TOPICS LIKE PARTITIONING, STORED PROCEDURES, AND TRIGGERS.

---

## TARGET AUDIENCE:

- **JOB SEEKERS:** CANDIDATES PREPARING FOR SQL INTERVIEWS IN TOP SOFTWARE COMPANIES.
- **STUDENTS:** COLLEGE STUDENTS LOOKING TO STRENGTHEN THEIR SQL SKILLS FOR LAB WORK AND EXAMS.
- **PROFESSIONALS:** DEVELOPERS AND ANALYSTS AIMING TO REFINE THEIR SQL EXPERTISE AND HANDLE COMPLEX DATA CHALLENGES.

## ABOUT THE AUTHOR

ANSHUMAN MISHRA, AN ACCOMPLISHED ACADEMIC AND EDUCATOR, HAS OVER 18 YEARS OF TEACHING EXPERIENCE AS AN ASSISTANT PROFESSOR IN COMPUTER SCIENCE. HE HOLDS AN M.TECH IN COMPUTER SCIENCE FROM THE PRESTIGIOUS BIRLA INSTITUTE OF TECHNOLOGY, MESRA. CURRENTLY SERVING AT DORANDA COLLEGE, RANCHI, HE SPECIALIZES IN PROGRAMMING LANGUAGES, SOFTWARE DEVELOPMENT, AND COMPUTER SKILLS, INSPIRING COUNTLESS STUDENTS WITH HIS PROFOUND KNOWLEDGE AND PRACTICAL INSIGHTS.

ANSHUMAN IS A PASSIONATE WRITER WITH EXPERTISE IN CREATING EDUCATIONAL RESOURCES FOR STUDENTS AND PROFESSIONALS. HIS BOOKS COVER TOPICS LIKE JAVA PROGRAMMING, SQL, OPERATING SYSTEMS, AND COMPETITIVE PROGRAMMING, REFLECTING HIS DEDICATION TO MAKING COMPLEX SUBJECTS ACCESSIBLE AND ENGAGING.

BEYOND ACADEMICS, ANSHUMAN IS A MOTIVATIONAL THINKER, A LOVER OF MYSTERIES, AND A STORYTELLER AT HEART. HE HAS AUTHORED WORKS RANGING FROM SELF-MOTIVATION GUIDES TO CHILDREN'S STORIES AND BOOKS DELVING INTO THE RICH HISTORY AND CULTURE OF JHARKHAND. HIS ABILITY TO WEAVE KNOWLEDGE WITH INSPIRATION MAKES HIS BOOKS A TREASURE FOR READERS OF ALL AGES.

**"Programs must be written for people to read, and only incidentally for machines to execute."**
— Harold Abelson & Gerald Jay Sussman, *Structure and Interpretation of Computer Programs*

Copyright Page

Title: **MASTERING SQL FOR INTERVIEWS AND BEYOND**

**Author: Anshuman Kumar Mishra**

## TOPICS

## CHAPTER-1

### 1. INTRODUCTION TO SQL

- What is SQL?
  - SQL (Structured Query Language) is a standard programming language designed for managing and manipulating relational databases. It is used to perform tasks such as querying, updating, and managing data.
  - SQL provides a uniform interface for interacting with data, making it easier for users to retrieve, modify, and analyze information.
- History and Evolution of SQL
  - SQL was initially developed in the 1970s by IBM researchers Donald D. Chamberlin and Raymond F. Boyce, as a part of the System R project.
  - The first commercial implementation of SQL was released by Oracle in 1979.
  - Over time, SQL became an ANSI (1986) and ISO (1987) standard, leading to widespread adoption.
  - Modern SQL has evolved to include support for JSON, XML, analytics, and other advanced features.
- Importance of SQL in Modern Databases
  - SQL is the backbone of almost every relational database management system (RDBMS) such as MySQL, PostgreSQL, SQL Server, and Oracle Database.
  - It is essential for data analysis, enabling businesses to extract meaningful insights from large datasets.
  - SQL integrates seamlessly with various programming languages, making it a critical skill for developers.
  - The language ensures data integrity and security through standardized query execution.

## Types of SQL Statements

SQL statements can be classified into four major categories based on their purpose: **DDL (Data Definition Language)**, **DML (Data Manipulation Language)**, **DCL (Data Control Language)**, and **TCL (Transaction Control Language)**. Each category serves a distinct function in managing a database.

---

## 1. DDL (Data Definition Language)

DDL statements are used to define, create, and modify the structure of database objects such as tables, indexes, and schemas.

*Key Features:*

- Defines the database schema.
- Operates on the structural level, not the data itself.

- Auto-commits changes, meaning that they are permanent.

*Common DDL Commands:*

1. **CREATE**: Used to create new database objects.
   - Example:

```
CREATE TABLE Employees (
    ID INT PRIMARY KEY,
    Name VARCHAR(50),
    Salary DECIMAL(10, 2)
);
```

2. **ALTER**: Used to modify existing database objects.
   - Example:

```
ALTER TABLE Employees ADD Department VARCHAR(50);
```

3. **DROP**: Deletes database objects permanently.
   - Example:

```
DROP TABLE Employees;
```

4. **TRUNCATE**: Removes all records from a table but keeps the structure intact.
   - Example:

```
TRUNCATE TABLE Employees;
```

---

## 2. DML (Data Manipulation Language)

DML statements deal with manipulating data stored in the database. These statements focus on retrieving, inserting, updating, or deleting data.

*Key Features:*

- Operates directly on the data.
- Changes are not auto-committed and can be controlled with TCL commands.

*Common DML Commands:*

1. **SELECT**: Retrieves data from a table.
   - Example:

```
SELECT * FROM Employees WHERE Salary > 50000;
```

2. **INSERT**: Adds new rows to a table.
   - Example:

```
INSERT INTO Employees (ID, Name, Salary) VALUES (1, 'John Doe',
60000);
```

3. **UPDATE**: Modifies existing data in a table.
   - Example:

     ```
     UPDATE Employees SET Salary = 70000 WHERE ID = 1;
     ```

4. **DELETE**: Removes rows from a table.
   - Example:

     ```
     DELETE FROM Employees WHERE ID = 1;
     ```

---

## 3. DCL (Data Control Language)

DCL statements are used to manage access and permissions to the database objects.

*Key Features:*

- Grants or restricts user access to database objects.
- Ensures security and control over data access.

*Common DCL Commands:*

1. **GRANT**: Provides permissions to users.
   - Example:

     ```
     GRANT SELECT, INSERT ON Employees TO User1;
     ```

2. **REVOKE**: Removes permissions from users.
   - Example:

     ```
     REVOKE INSERT ON Employees FROM User1;
     ```

---

## 4. TCL (Transaction Control Language)

TCL statements are used to manage database transactions, ensuring data integrity and consistency.

*Key Features:*

- Ensures that a sequence of DML operations is treated as a single unit.
- Allows control over whether changes are committed or rolled back.

*Common TCL Commands:*

1. **COMMIT**: Saves all changes made in the transaction to the database.
   - Example:

     ```
     COMMIT;
     ```

2. **ROLLBACK**: Reverts changes made during the current transaction.
   - Example:

     ```
     ROLLBACK;
     ```

3. **SAVEPOINT**: Sets a point within a transaction to which you can roll back.
   - Example:

     ```
     SAVEPOINT Save1;
     ```

4. **SET TRANSACTION**: Configures transaction properties such as isolation level.
   - Example:

     ```
     SET TRANSACTION READ WRITE;
     ```

---

## Summary Table

| Category | Purpose | Examples | Key Features |
|---|---|---|---|
| **DDL** | Defines database structure and schema. | CREATE, ALTER, DROP | Auto-commits changes, permanent modifications. |
| **DML** | Manipulates data stored in the database. | SELECT, INSERT, UPDATE, DELETE | Changes are not auto-committed. |
| **DCL** | Manages access control and permissions. | GRANT, REVOKE | Ensures security and user access control. |
| **TCL** | Controls database transactions. | COMMIT, ROLLBACK, SAVEPOINT | Maintains data integrity and consistency. |

---

This classification helps database administrators and developers effectively manage database systems by organizing tasks based on their purpose.

- Overview of SQL Tools and Interfaces
    - Command-Line Tools: Tools like MySQL CLI and psql provide direct access to databases via SQL commands.
    - GUI-Based Tools: Applications such as MySQL Workbench, pgAdmin, and SQL Server Management Studio (SSMS) offer graphical interfaces for writing and executing SQL queries.
    - Integrated Development Environments (IDEs): Tools like DataGrip and dbForge Studio provide advanced features for database development and administration.
    - Web-Based Platforms: Online platforms like phpMyAdmin and Adminer allow users to manage databases via a browser.

## CHAPTER-2

## FUNDAMENTALS OF RELATIONAL DATABASES

Relational databases form the backbone of many modern applications, offering a structured way to store and retrieve data efficiently. They are based on the principles of relational algebra and are built around the concept of tables.

---

*Relational Database Concepts*

1. **Definition**:
   - A relational database is a type of database that organizes data into one or more tables (also called relations), where each table consists of rows and columns.
   - It follows the principles of relational algebra, ensuring data is structured and can be queried using SQL.
2. **Key Characteristics**:
   - **Structured Data**: Data is stored in tables with predefined schemas.
   - **Data Integrity**: Ensures consistency and accuracy through constraints like primary and foreign keys.
   - **Relationships**: Tables can be linked using keys, enabling data interconnection.
3. **Benefits**:
   - Easy data retrieval using SQL.
   - High data accuracy and consistency.
   - Flexibility in querying and reporting.

---

## Understanding Tables, Rows, and Columns in Relational Databases

*1. Tables*

- A **table** is the fundamental building block of a relational database.
- It organizes data into rows and columns, where each table represents a specific entity or concept.
- For example:
  - An "Employees" table contains data about employees.
  - A "Products" table stores information about products.

*Example of a Table*

Here is an example of an "Employees" table:

| ID | Name | Department | Salary |
|---|---|---|---|
| 1 | John Doe | HR | 50000 |
| 2 | Jane Smith | IT | 60000 |
| 3 | Alice Johnson | Marketing | 55000 |

### *Graphical Representation of a Table*

The graphical representation can be visualized as a grid-like structure where:

- **Columns** are vertical headers (e.g., ID, Name, Department, Salary).
- **Rows** are horizontal entries, each representing a record.

---

### *2. Rows (Tuples)*

- A **row** in a table corresponds to a single **record** or **entry**.
- Each row contains data about a specific instance of the entity represented by the table.

### *Example*

- In the "Employees" table:
  - The first row (Tuple 1) contains details of **John Doe**:
    - ID = 1, Name = John Doe, Department = HR, Salary = 50000.

### *Graphical Representation of Rows*

Each row is visually represented as a single horizontal line in the table:

```
| ID: 1 | Name: John Doe | Department: HR | Salary: 50000 |
```

---

### *3. Columns (Attributes)*

- A **column** represents a specific **attribute** or **property** of the entity.
- Each column holds the same type of data for all rows.

### *Example*

- In the "Employees" table:
  - The **ID** column contains unique identifiers for employees.
  - The **Name** column contains their names.
  - The **Department** column specifies the department they work in.
  - The **Salary** column lists their salaries.

*Graphical Representation of Columns*

Columns are depicted as vertical divisions:

```
| **ID** | **Name** | **Department** | **Salary** |
```

---

*4. Schema*

- The **schema** defines the structure of a table, specifying the columns and their data types.
- It acts as a blueprint for what kind of data the table can store.

*Example Schema for the "Employees" Table*

- **ID**: Integer (e.g., 1, 2, 3)
- **Name**: String (e.g., "John Doe", "Jane Smith")
- **Department**: String (e.g., "HR", "IT")
- **Salary**: Decimal (e.g., 50000, 60000)

*Graphical Representation of Schema*

The schema can be visualized as a column header with data types:

```
| **ID (Integer)** | **Name (String)** | **Department (String)** | **Salary
(Decimal)** |
```

---

## Complete Graphical Diagram

Below is a graphical diagram combining all the elements:

```
Table: Employees
+----+----------------+------------+--------+
| ID | Name           | Department | Salary |
+----+----------------+------------+--------+
|  1 | John Doe       | HR         | 50000  |
|  2 | Jane Smith     | IT         | 60000  |
|  3 | Alice Johnson  | Marketing  | 55000  |
+----+----------------+------------+--------+

Schema:
ID: Integer
Name: String
Department: String
Salary: Decimal
```

---

## Primary and Foreign Keys in Relational Databases

In relational databases, keys are crucial for maintaining data integrity, ensuring that records are unique, and establishing relationships between different tables. There are mainly two types of keys discussed here: **Primary Keys** and **Foreign Keys**. Let's go through both in detail, along with their rules and how they interact.

---

## 1. Primary Key

*Definition:*

- A **Primary Key** is a column (or a set of columns) that **uniquely identifies each row** in a table.
- It ensures that each record in a table can be uniquely identified by its primary key value, which avoids duplication.

*Key Characteristics:*

- **Uniqueness**: Every value in a primary key column must be unique across all rows.
- **Non-null**: The primary key cannot have **NULL** values because it needs to uniquely identify each row.

*Example:*

Consider the "Employees" table below:

| ID | Name | Department | Salary |
|---|---|---|---|
| 1 | John Doe | HR | 50000 |
| 2 | Jane Smith | IT | 60000 |
| 3 | Alice Johnson | Marketing | 55000 |

In this table:

- The **ID** column is the **primary key** because it uniquely identifies each employee. Each employee has a unique ID number, and no two employees share the same ID.

*Rules of Primary Key:*

1. **Uniqueness**: No two rows in the table can have the same value in the primary key column.
2. **Non-null**: The primary key column cannot contain NULL values. Every row must have a valid, unique primary key.

## 2. Foreign Key

*Definition:*

- A **Foreign Key** is a column (or a set of columns) in one table that **refers to the primary key** in another table.
- It creates a **link** between the two tables, establishing a relationship between the records in them.

*Key Characteristics:*

- A foreign key in a table points to the primary key in another table.
- It ensures that values in the foreign key column must match values in the primary key column of the referenced table, thereby maintaining referential integrity.

*Example:*

Consider the following two tables: "Employees" and "Departments".

**Employees Table**:

| ID | Name | Department_ID | Salary |
|---|---|---|---|
| 1 | John Doe | 1 | 50000 |
| 2 | Jane Smith | 2 | 60000 |
| 3 | Alice Johnson | 1 | 55000 |

**Departments Table**:

| Department_ID | Department_Name |
|---|---|
| 1 | HR |
| 2 | IT |

In this example:

- In the **Employees** table, the **Department_ID** column is a **foreign key** because it refers to the **Department_ID** primary key in the **Departments** table.
- This foreign key ensures that the **Department_ID** in the "Employees" table must match a valid **Department_ID** from the "Departments" table (1 for HR, 2 for IT).

*Example Schema for the "Departments" Table:*

- **Department_ID**: Integer (Primary Key)
- **Department_Name**: String

The foreign key relationship allows us to link employees to their respective departments.

---

## 3. Relationship Between Keys

The interaction between **primary keys** and **foreign keys** helps to establish relationships between tables. These relationships can be classified as:

*One-to-One (1:1) Relationship:*

- **Definition**: A single record in one table is related to a single record in another table.
- **Example**:
  - Consider a scenario where each **employee** has a **unique office** (one office per employee). The "Employee" table would have a **primary key** (Employee_ID), and the "Office" table would have a **foreign key** pointing back to Employee_ID.

*One-to-Many (1:N) Relationship:*

- **Definition**: A single record in one table can relate to multiple records in another table, but each record in the second table can relate to only one record in the first table.
- **Example**:
  - In the **Employees** table, the **Department_ID** is a **foreign key** that refers to the **Departments** table. A **single department** (e.g., HR) can have **multiple employees**, but each **employee** belongs to only **one department**.

*Many-to-Many (M:N) Relationship:*

- **Definition**: A single record in one table can be related to multiple records in another table, and vice versa.
- **Example**:
  - Consider a **Students** table and a **Courses** table. A student can enroll in multiple courses, and each course can have multiple students. To manage this, a **junction table** (e.g., **Enrollments**) is used, which contains **foreign keys** referencing both the **Students** and **Courses** tables.

---

## Graphical Representation

*Primary Key Example (One-to-One or One-to-Many):*

```
Employees Table (Primary Key: ID)
+----+----------------+-------------------+--------+
| ID | Name           | Department_ID     | Salary |
+----+----------------+-------------------+--------+
|  1 | John Doe       | 1                 | 50000  |
|  2 | Jane Smith     | 2                 | 60000  |
|  3 | Alice Johnson  | 1                 | 55000  |
+----+----------------+-------------------+--------+

Departments Table (Primary Key: Department_ID)
+--------------------+---------------------+
| Department_ID      | Department_Name     |
+--------------------+---------------------+
| 1                  | HR                  |
| 2                  | IT                  |
+--------------------+---------------------+
```

- **Foreign Key (Department_ID)** in "Employees" table points to **Primary Key (Department_ID)** in the "Departments" table.

---

*Many-to-Many Relationship (Junction Table Example):*

```
Students Table (Primary Key: Student_ID)
+------------+------------+
| Student_ID | Name       |
+------------+------------+
| 101        | Alice      |
| 102        | Bob        |
+------------+------------+

Courses Table (Primary Key: Course_ID)
+------------+-------------+
| Course_ID  | Course_Name |
+------------+-------------+
| 201        | Math        |
| 202        | Science     |
+------------+-------------+

Enrollments Table (Junction Table with Foreign Keys)
+------------+------------+
| Student_ID | Course_ID  |
+------------+------------+
| 101        | 201        |
| 101        | 202        |
| 102        | 202        |
+------------+------------+
```

- The **Enrollments** table manages the many-to-many relationship between **Students** and **Courses** using **foreign keys**.

*Entity-Relationship (ER) Model*

1. **Definition**:
   - The ER model is a conceptual representation of the data and relationships within a database.
   - It is typically illustrated using an ER diagram.
2. **Components**:
   - **Entities**: Represent objects or concepts, such as "Employee" or "Department."
   - **Attributes**: Properties of entities, such as "Name" or "Salary."
   - **Relationships**: Define how entities are connected, e.g., an "Employee" belongs to a "Department."
3. **Diagram Symbols**:
   - Rectangles: Represent entities.
   - Ovals: Represent attributes.
   - Diamonds: Represent relationships.
4. **Example ER Diagram**:

```
Employee ---- belongs_to ---- Department
```

---

## Relational Algebra Basics

Relational algebra is a formal query language used for manipulating and retrieving data in relational databases. It serves as the theoretical foundation for SQL (Structured Query Language) operations and defines the basic operations that can be applied to relations (tables). The goal of relational algebra is to provide a set of operations that can express any query on a relational database.

---

## 1. Definition of Relational Algebra

- **Relational Algebra** is a procedural query language that operates on relations (tables) and produces a new relation as a result.
- It is based on a set of operations that work on relations and return results that are themselves relations. These operations are used to query, update, and combine data from multiple tables.
- **Key Concept**: In relational algebra, the main goal is to manipulate and retrieve data using **relations** (tables) through different operations, just like SQL is used in practice.

---

## 2. Operations in Relational Algebra

The operations in relational algebra can be divided into **basic operations** and **derived operations**. Below are the fundamental operations:

*a. Selection (σ)*

- **Definition**: The selection operation filters rows from a table based on a given condition. It selects the rows that satisfy a condition, effectively **reducing** the number of rows in the resulting relation.
- **Symbol**: σ (sigma)

**Example**:

- σ(Salary > 50000)(Employees)

This operation selects all rows from the **Employees** table where the **Salary** is greater than 50,000. The result will be a relation that includes only employees with a salary greater than 50,000.

| ID | Name | Department | Salary |
|---|---|---|---|
| 2 | Jane Smith | IT | 60000 |

*b. Projection (π)*

- **Definition**: The projection operation is used to select specific columns from a relation. It eliminates the other columns and returns only the columns of interest.
- **Symbol**: π (pi)

**Example**:

- π(Name, Salary)(Employees)

This operation selects only the **Name** and **Salary** columns from the **Employees** table. The result will be a relation with only those two attributes:

| Name | Salary |
|---|---|
| John Doe | 50000 |
| Jane Smith | 60000 |
| Alice Johnson | 55000 |

*c. Union (∪)*

- **Definition**: The union operation combines the rows of two relations, excluding duplicates. Both relations must have the same set of columns (i.e., the same arity).
- **Symbol**: ∪ (union)

**Example**:

- Employees_1 ∪ Employees_2

This operation combines the rows from two **Employees** relations. The result will contain all distinct rows from both tables.

*d. Set Difference (-)*

- **Definition**: The set difference operation returns the rows that are present in one relation but not in another. This operation finds records that exist in the first table but not in the second.
- **Symbol**: - (set difference)

**Example**:

- Employees - Retired_Employees

This operation will return the rows from **Employees** that do not exist in the **Retired_Employees** relation. In other words, it finds all employees who are not retired.

*e. Cartesian Product (×)*

- **Definition**: The Cartesian product operation combines every row of one relation with every row of another relation. It produces a new relation containing all possible combinations of rows from both relations.
- **Symbol**: × (cross product)

**Example**:

- Employees × Departments

This operation combines each row of the **Employees** table with every row of the **Departments** table. If **Employees** has 3 rows and **Departments** has 2 rows, the result will have 3 × 2 = 6 rows.

| ID | Name | Department | Salary | Department_ID | Department_Name |
|---|---|---|---|---|---|
| 1 | John Doe | HR | 50000 | 1 | HR |
| 1 | John Doe | HR | 50000 | 2 | IT |
| 2 | Jane Smith | IT | 60000 | 1 | HR |
| 2 | Jane Smith | IT | 60000 | 2 | IT |
| 3 | Alice Johnson | Marketing | 55000 | 1 | HR |

| ID | Name | Department | Salary | Department_ID | Department_Name |
|---|---|---|---|---|---|
| 3 | Alice Johnson | Marketing | 55000 | 2 | IT |

*f. Join (⋈)*

- **Definition**: The join operation combines rows from two relations based on a common attribute. The most common type of join is the **inner join**, which only includes rows that have matching values in the joined columns.
- **Symbol**: ⋈ (join)

**Example**:

- Employees ⋈ Departments

This operation joins the **Employees** and **Departments** tables on the matching **Department_ID** column. The result is a combined table that includes only the employees with their corresponding department details.

| ID | Name | Department | Salary | Department_Name |
|---|---|---|---|---|
| 1 | John Doe | HR | 50000 | HR |
| 2 | Jane Smith | IT | 60000 | IT |
| 3 | Alice Johnson | Marketing | 55000 | HR |

*g. Rename (ρ)*

- **Definition**: The rename operation is used to give a new name to a relation or its attributes. This operation is often useful when we need to rename tables or columns to avoid confusion in complex queries.
- **Symbol**: ρ (rho)

**Example**:

- ρ(Employees_Updated)(Employees)

This operation renames the **Employees** relation to **Employees_Updated**, essentially giving it a new alias for use in further operations.

---

## 3. Relational Query

A **relational query** involves using combinations of these basic operations to extract, manipulate, and combine data across one or more relations. Queries are composed of one or more operations to filter rows, select columns, join tables, or even combine results from different tables.

*Example of a Relational Query:*

To get the names and salaries of employees who work in the **HR** department and have a salary greater than **50,000**, the relational algebra query could be written as:

- **σ(Department = 'HR' AND Salary > 50000)(π(Name, Salary)(Employees))**

This query performs:

1. **Projection (π)** to select the **Name** and **Salary** columns from the **Employees** table.
2. **Selection (σ)** to filter the results based on the conditions that the **Department** is 'HR' and **Salary** is greater than 50,000.

    ○

---

## Summary

Relational databases provide a systematic approach to store and retrieve structured data. Understanding the concepts of tables, rows, columns, keys, and relationships helps in designing effective database schemas. The entity-relationship model aids in conceptualizing data, while relational algebra provides the theoretical foundation for database queries. These fundamentals are essential for leveraging the full power of relational databases in real-world applications.

# CHAPTER-3

## DATA RETRIEVAL: SELECT QUERIES

The **SELECT** statement in SQL is used to retrieve data from one or more tables in a database. It is the most commonly used statement for querying and extracting data. Let's break down the various components and techniques used to write efficient SELECT queries.

---

### 1. Writing Basic SELECT Statements

The **SELECT** statement is used to query data from a table. It specifies which columns of data to retrieve. The most basic form of the SELECT query retrieves all the columns from a table.

*Syntax:*

```
SELECT column1, column2, ...
FROM table_name;
```

- **column1, column2, ...**: Specifies the columns to retrieve. You can select one or more columns.
- **table_name**: The name of the table from which the data will be retrieved.

*Example:*

To select the **Name** and **Salary** columns from an **Employees** table:

```
SELECT Name, Salary
FROM Employees;
```

This query will return the following result from the **Employees** table:

| Name | Salary |
|---|---|
| John Doe | 50000 |
| Jane Smith | 60000 |
| Alice Johnson | 55000 |

*Selecting All Columns:*

To retrieve all columns from the **Employees** table:

```
SELECT *
FROM Employees;
```

The `*` symbol retrieves all columns available in the table.

## 2. Using WHERE Clause for Filtering

The **WHERE** clause is used to filter records based on specific conditions. It allows you to retrieve only the rows that meet certain criteria.

*Syntax:*

```
SELECT column1, column2, ...
FROM table_name
WHERE condition;
```

- **condition**: The condition is used to filter rows based on specific criteria (e.g., greater than, less than, equal to, etc.).

*Example:*

To select all employees whose salary is greater than 50,000:

```
SELECT Name, Salary
FROM Employees
WHERE Salary > 50000;
```

This query will return the following result:

| Name | Salary |
|---|---|
| Jane Smith | 60000 |

*Example with Multiple Conditions:*

You can also use logical operators like **AND**, **OR**, and **NOT** to combine multiple conditions. For example, to retrieve employees who are from the **IT** department and have a salary greater than 50,000:

```
SELECT Name, Department, Salary
FROM Employees
WHERE Department = 'IT' AND Salary > 50000;
```

---

## 3. Sorting Results with ORDER BY

The **ORDER BY** clause is used to sort the results of a query in ascending or descending order. By default, the sorting is done in **ascending order**, but you can use the **DESC** keyword to sort in **descending order**.

*Syntax:*

```
SELECT column1, column2, ...
FROM table_name
```

```
ORDER BY column1 [ASC | DESC], column2 [ASC | DESC], ...;
```

- **column1, column2, ...**: Columns by which you want to sort the result.
- **ASC**: Sorts the results in ascending order (default).
- **DESC**: Sorts the results in descending order.

*Example:*

To retrieve employees' names and salaries sorted by salary in descending order:

```
SELECT Name, Salary
FROM Employees
ORDER BY Salary DESC;
```

This will sort the results by **Salary** from highest to lowest:

| Name | Salary |
|---|---|
| Jane Smith | 60000 |
| Alice Johnson | 55000 |
| John Doe | 50000 |

*Example with Multiple Sorting:*

You can also sort by more than one column. For example, to sort employees first by **Department** and then by **Salary** in descending order:

```
SELECT Name, Department, Salary
FROM Employees
ORDER BY Department ASC, Salary DESC;
```

---

## 4. Limiting Results with LIMIT and OFFSET

The **LIMIT** clause is used to restrict the number of rows returned by a query. It is often used when you want to return only a specific number of records.

The **OFFSET** clause is used in conjunction with **LIMIT** to skip a specific number of rows before starting to return the rows.

*Syntax:*

```
SELECT column1, column2, ...
FROM table_name
LIMIT number_of_rows OFFSET number_of_rows_to_skip;
```

- **LIMIT number_of_rows**: Specifies the maximum number of rows to return.
- **OFFSET number_of_rows_to_skip**: Skips a specified number of rows before beginning to return the results.

*Example:*

To retrieve the top 2 highest-paid employees:

```
SELECT Name, Salary
FROM Employees
ORDER BY Salary DESC
LIMIT 2;
```

This will return the top 2 employees with the highest salaries:

| Name | Salary |
|---|---|
| Jane Smith | 60000 |
| Alice Johnson | 55000 |

*Example with OFFSET:*

To skip the first 2 rows and then return the next 2 rows:

```
SELECT Name, Salary
FROM Employees
ORDER BY Salary DESC
LIMIT 2 OFFSET 2;
```

This will return the next 2 employees after skipping the first 2:

| Name | Salary |
|---|---|
| John Doe | 50000 |
| Alice Johnson | 55000 |

---

## 5. Distinct Values with DISTINCT

The **DISTINCT** keyword is used to remove duplicate values from the result set. It ensures that only unique records are returned.

*Syntax:*

```
SELECT DISTINCT column1, column2, ...
FROM table_name;
```

*Example:*

To retrieve a list of distinct **Departments** from the **Employees** table:

```
SELECT DISTINCT Department
FROM Employees;
```

This will return only unique department names, without duplicates:

| Department |
|---|
| HR |
| IT |
| Marketing |

---

## Graphical Diagram

Let's visualize a query example to better understand how SELECT, WHERE, ORDER BY, and DISTINCT work together.

Imagine we have the following **Employees** table:

| ID | Name | Department | Salary |
|---|---|---|---|
| 1 | John Doe | HR | 50000 |
| 2 | Jane Smith | IT | 60000 |
| 3 | Alice Johnson | HR | 55000 |
| 4 | Bob Brown | IT | 55000 |
| 5 | Charlie White | Marketing | 70000 |

*Query Example:*

```
SELECT DISTINCT Department
FROM Employees
WHERE Salary > 50000
ORDER BY Department ASC;
```

- **Step 1**: **WHERE** filters employees with salaries greater than 50,000.
- **Step 2**: **DISTINCT** removes duplicates from the result set.
- **Step 3**: **ORDER BY** sorts the departments in ascending order.

**Result**:

| **Department** |
|---|
| IT |
| Marketing |

This query shows only the unique departments of employees who earn more than 50,000, sorted in ascending order.

## 1. Basic SELECT Statement

**Task**: Retrieve all columns from the **Employees** table.

*Query:*

```
SELECT * FROM Employees;
```

*Explanation:*

This query retrieves all rows and columns from the **Employees** table.

---

## 2. Selecting Specific Columns

**Task**: Retrieve only the **Name** and **Salary** of employees.

*Query:*

```
sql
SELECT Name, Salary FROM Employees;
```

*Explanation:*

This query retrieves only the **Name** and **Salary** columns from the **Employees** table.

---

## 3. Using WHERE Clause for Filtering

**Task**: Retrieve employees whose **Salary** is greater than 60,000.

*Query:*

```
SELECT Name, Salary FROM Employees
WHERE Salary > 60000;
```

*Explanation:*

This query filters employees whose salary exceeds 60,000 and retrieves their names and salaries.

---

## 4. Using WHERE Clause with Multiple Conditions (AND)

**Task**: Retrieve employees who are in the **IT** department and have a **Salary** greater than 50,000.

*Query:*

```
SELECT Name, Department, Salary FROM Employees
WHERE Department = 'IT' AND Salary > 50000;
```

*Explanation:*

This query retrieves employees from the **IT** department with a salary greater than 50,000.

---

## 5. Using WHERE Clause with Multiple Conditions (OR)

**Task**: Retrieve employees who are in the **HR** department or have a **Salary** greater than 60,000.

*Query:*

```
SELECT Name, Department, Salary FROM Employees
WHERE Department = 'HR' OR Salary > 60000;
```

*Explanation:*

This query retrieves employees who are either in the **HR** department or have a salary above 60,000.

---

## 6. Sorting Results with ORDER BY (Ascending)

**Task**: Retrieve employees' **Name** and **Salary**, sorted by **Salary** in ascending order.

*Query:*

```
SELECT Name, Salary FROM Employees
ORDER BY Salary ASC;
```

*Explanation:*

This query retrieves employee names and their salaries, sorted from lowest to highest salary.

## 7. Sorting Results with ORDER BY (Descending)

**Task**: Retrieve employees' **Name** and **Salary**, sorted by **Salary** in descending order.

*Query:*
```
SELECT Name, Salary FROM Employees
ORDER BY Salary DESC;
```
*Explanation:*

This query retrieves employee names and their salaries, sorted from highest to lowest salary.

---

## 8. Limiting Results with LIMIT

**Task**: Retrieve the top 3 highest-paid employees' **Name** and **Salary**.

*Query:*
```
SELECT Name, Salary FROM Employees
ORDER BY Salary DESC
LIMIT 3;
```
*Explanation:*

This query retrieves the top 3 highest-paid employees sorted in descending order of salary.

---

## 9. Limiting Results with OFFSET

**Task**: Retrieve employees' **Name** and **Salary** from row 4 to row 6.

*Query:*
```
SELECT Name, Salary FROM Employees
ORDER BY Salary DESC
LIMIT 3 OFFSET 3;
```
*Explanation:*

This query skips the first 3 rows (highest salaries) and retrieves employees from row 4 to row 6.

---

## 10. Using DISTINCT to Retrieve Unique Values

**Task**: Retrieve a list of unique **Departments** from the **Employees** table.

*Query:*

```
SELECT DISTINCT Department FROM Employees;
```

*Explanation:*

This query retrieves unique department names without duplicates from the **Employees** table.

---

## Summary Table:

| Query Number | Description | SQL Query |
|---|---|---|
| 1 | Basic SELECT | `SELECT * FROM Employees;` |
| 2 | Selecting Specific Columns | `SELECT Name, Salary FROM Employees;` |
| 3 | Filtering with WHERE (Salary > 60000) | `SELECT Name, Salary FROM Employees WHERE Salary > 60000;` |
| 4 | Multiple Conditions (AND) | `SELECT Name, Department, Salary FROM Employees WHERE Department = 'IT' AND Salary > 50000;` |
| 5 | Multiple Conditions (OR) | `SELECT Name, Department, Salary FROM Employees WHERE Department = 'HR' OR Salary > 60000;` |
| 6 | Sorting by Salary (Ascending) | `SELECT Name, Salary FROM Employees ORDER BY Salary ASC;` |
| 7 | Sorting by Salary (Descending) | `SELECT Name, Salary FROM Employees ORDER BY Salary DESC;` |
| 8 | Limiting Results with LIMIT | `SELECT Name, Salary FROM Employees ORDER BY Salary DESC LIMIT 3;` |
| 9 | Limiting Results with OFFSET | `SELECT Name, Salary FROM Employees ORDER BY Salary DESC LIMIT 3 OFFSET 3;` |
| 10 | Distinct Departments | `SELECT DISTINCT Department FROM Employees;` |

These examples cover various scenarios you may encounter when retrieving data using **SELECT** queries. You can modify these queries according to the structure of your tables and requirements.

## 11. Using IN for Multiple Conditions

**Task**: Retrieve employees who belong to either the **HR** or **IT** department.

*Query:*

```
SELECT Name, Department FROM Employees
WHERE Department IN ('HR', 'IT');
```

*Explanation:*

This query retrieves employees from either the **HR** or **IT** department using the **IN** condition to specify multiple values.

---

## 12. Using LIKE for Pattern Matching

**Task**: Retrieve employees whose **Name** starts with the letter "J".

*Query:*

```
SELECT Name FROM Employees
WHERE Name LIKE 'J%';
```

*Explanation:*

This query uses the **LIKE** operator with the pattern `'J%'` to find all employees whose names start with "J".

---

## 13. Using BETWEEN for Range Filtering

**Task**: Retrieve employees with a **Salary** between 50,000 and 70,000.

*Query:*

```
SELECT Name, Salary FROM Employees
WHERE Salary BETWEEN 50000 AND 70000;
```

*Explanation:*

This query retrieves employees whose salaries fall within the specified range using the **BETWEEN** operator.

---

## 14. Using AND with NOT for Excluding Values

**Task**: Retrieve employees who are not in the **HR** department and whose **Salary** is greater than 50,000.

*Query:*

```
SELECT Name, Department, Salary FROM Employees
WHERE Department != 'HR' AND Salary > 50000;
```

*Explanation:*

This query excludes employees from the **HR** department and filters employees with salaries greater than 50,000 using **AND** and **!=**.

---

## 15. Aggregate Function: COUNT()

**Task**: Retrieve the total number of employees in each department.

*Query:*

```
SELECT Department, COUNT(*) AS Total_Employees FROM Employees
GROUP BY Department;
```

*Explanation:*

This query counts the number of employees in each department using the **COUNT()** aggregate function and groups the result by department.

---

## 16. Aggregate Function: AVG()

**Task**: Retrieve the average salary of employees in the **IT** department.

*Query:*

```
SELECT AVG(Salary) AS Average_Salary FROM Employees
WHERE Department = 'IT';
```

*Explanation:*

This query calculates the average salary of employees in the **IT** department using the **AVG()** function.

---

## 17. Using GROUP BY with HAVING

**Task**: Retrieve departments with more than 5 employees.

*Query:*

```
SELECT Department, COUNT(*) AS Employee_Count FROM Employees
GROUP BY Department
HAVING COUNT(*) > 5;
```

*Explanation:*

This query groups the employees by department and retrieves only those departments where the number of employees is greater than 5 using the **HAVING** clause.

---

## 18. Joining Two Tables (INNER JOIN)

**Task**: Retrieve employee names along with their department names by joining the **Employees** and **Departments** tables.

*Query:*

```
SELECT Employees.Name, Departments.Department_Name
FROM Employees
INNER JOIN Departments ON Employees.Department_ID =
Departments.Department_ID;
```

*Explanation:*

This query retrieves employee names and their corresponding department names by joining the **Employees** and **Departments** tables on the **Department_ID**.

---

## 19. LEFT JOIN to Include Unmatched Rows

**Task**: Retrieve all employees and their department names, even if the employee doesn't belong to any department.

*Query:*

```
SELECT Employees.Name, Departments.Department_Name
FROM Employees
LEFT JOIN Departments ON Employees.Department_ID = Departments.Department_ID;
```

*Explanation:*

This query retrieves all employees and their department names, including employees without a department, using a **LEFT JOIN**.

---

## 20. Using Subquery in SELECT

**Task**: Retrieve employee names and their salary along with the maximum salary in the company.

*Query:*

```
SELECT Name, Salary, (SELECT MAX(Salary) FROM Employees) AS Max_Salary
FROM Employees;
```

*Explanation:*

This query retrieves employee names and salaries, along with the maximum salary in the company. The subquery calculates the maximum salary for the entire **Employees** table.

---

## Summary Table:

| Query Number | Description | SQL Query |
|---|---|---|
| 1 | Using IN for Multiple Conditions | `SELECT Name, Department FROM Employees WHERE Department IN ('HR', 'IT');` |
| 2 | Using LIKE for Pattern Matching | `SELECT Name FROM Employees WHERE Name LIKE 'J%';` |
| 3 | Using BETWEEN for Range Filtering | `SELECT Name, Salary FROM Employees WHERE Salary BETWEEN 50000 AND 70000;` |
| 4 | Using AND with NOT for Excluding Values | `SELECT Name, Department, Salary FROM Employees WHERE Department != 'HR' AND Salary > 50000;` |
| 5 | Aggregate Function: COUNT() | `SELECT Department, COUNT(*) AS Total_Employees FROM Employees GROUP BY Department;` |
| 6 | Aggregate Function: AVG() | `SELECT AVG(Salary) AS Average_Salary FROM Employees WHERE Department = 'IT';` |
| 7 | Using GROUP BY with HAVING | `SELECT Department, COUNT(*) AS Employee_Count FROM Employees GROUP BY Department HAVING COUNT(*) > 5;` |
| 8 | Joining Two Tables (INNER JOIN) | `SELECT Employees.Name, Departments.Department_Name FROM Employees INNER JOIN Departments ON Employees.Department_ID = Departments.Department_ID;` |

| Query Number | Description | SQL Query |
|---|---|---|
| 9 | LEFT JOIN to Include Unmatched Rows | `SELECT Employees.Name, Departments.Department_Name FROM Employees LEFT JOIN Departments ON Employees.Department_ID = Departments.Department_ID;` |
| 10 | Using Subquery in SELECT | `SELECT Name, Salary, (SELECT MAX(Salary) FROM Employees) AS Max_Salary FROM Employees;` |

These additional examples further cover practical SQL queries for data retrieval, including filtering, aggregation, joining, and working with subqueries. These queries can be adapted to your specific database structure and requirements.

---

## Conclusion

The **SELECT** query in SQL is a powerful tool for data retrieval. By combining operations like **WHERE**, **ORDER BY**, **LIMIT**, and **DISTINCT**, you can fine-tune your data retrieval to meet specific requirements. These SQL components help you filter, sort, limit, and remove duplicates in the data, making the process of querying databases efficient and effective.

# CHAPTER-4

## SQL FUNCTIONS AND OPERATORS

SQL provides a variety of functions and operators to help you manipulate and query data in more advanced and flexible ways. These functions can be categorized into **aggregate functions**, **string functions**, **date and time functions**, **logical operators**, and **arithmetic operators**. Below is a detailed explanation of each category.

---

### 1. Aggregate Functions

Aggregate functions perform a calculation on a set of values and return a single value. These are primarily used in conjunction with the **GROUP BY** clause to group rows that have the same values in specified columns.

*SUM():*

The **SUM()** function returns the total sum of a numeric column.

**Example**:

```
SELECT SUM(Salary) AS Total_Salary FROM Employees;
```

**Explanation**: This query calculates the total salary of all employees.

*AVG():*

The **AVG()** function returns the average (mean) value of a numeric column.

**Example**:

```
SELECT AVG(Salary) AS Average_Salary FROM Employees;
```

**Explanation**: This query calculates the average salary of all employees.

*COUNT():*

The **COUNT()** function counts the number of rows in a table, or the number of rows that match a condition.

**Example**:

```
SELECT COUNT(*) AS Employee_Count FROM Employees;
```

**Explanation**: This query counts the total number of employees.

*MIN():*

The **MIN()** function returns the smallest value in a numeric, string, or date column.

**Example**:

```
SELECT MIN(Salary) AS Minimum_Salary FROM Employees;
```

**Explanation**: This query finds the lowest salary among all employees.

*MAX():*

The **MAX()** function returns the largest value in a numeric, string, or date column.

**Example**:

```
SELECT MAX(Salary) AS Maximum_Salary FROM Employees;
```

**Explanation**: This query finds the highest salary among all employees.

---

## 2. String Functions

String functions allow you to manipulate text values stored in string columns (e.g., names, addresses, descriptions).

*CONCAT():*

The **CONCAT()** function is used to combine two or more strings into a single string.

**Example**:

```
SELECT CONCAT(FirstName, ' ', LastName) AS FullName FROM Employees;
```

**Explanation**: This query concatenates the **FirstName** and **LastName** columns to create a **FullName**.

*SUBSTRING():*

The **SUBSTRING()** function is used to extract a substring from a string.

**Example**:

```
SELECT SUBSTRING(Email, 1, 5) AS Short_Email FROM Employees;
```

**Explanation**: This query extracts the first 5 characters of the **Email** column.

*LENGTH():*

The **LENGTH()** function returns the length of a string (i.e., the number of characters in the string).

**Example**:

```
SELECT LENGTH(Name) AS Name_Length FROM Employees;
```

**Explanation**: This query returns the number of characters in the **Name** column.

---

## 3. Date and Time Functions

SQL provides several functions to manipulate date and time values. These are useful for performing calculations, comparisons, and formatting.

*NOW():*

The **NOW()** function returns the current date and time based on the system's clock.

**Example**:

```
SELECT NOW() AS Current_DateTime;
```

**Explanation**: This query returns the current date and time when the query is executed.

*DATE_ADD():*

The **DATE_ADD()** function adds a specified interval (such as days, months, or years) to a date.

**Example**:

```
SELECT DATE_ADD(HireDate, INTERVAL 1 YEAR) AS OneYearLater FROM Employees;
```

**Explanation**: This query adds one year to the **HireDate** of each employee.

*DATE_DIFF():*

The **DATE_DIFF()** function calculates the difference between two dates and returns the result as an integer (number of days).

**Example**:

```
SELECT DATEDIFF(CURRENT_DATE, HireDate) AS Days_Employed FROM Employees;
```

**Explanation**: This query calculates the number of days an employee has been employed by subtracting the **HireDate** from the current date.

---

## 4. Logical Operators

Logical operators allow you to combine multiple conditions in SQL queries. These operators are used to filter results based on multiple criteria.

*AND:*

The **AND** operator is used to combine two or more conditions, and the result is true only if all conditions are true.

**Example**:

```
SELECT Name FROM Employees
WHERE Department = 'HR' AND Salary > 50000;
```

**Explanation**: This query retrieves employees who are in the **HR** department and have a salary greater than 50,000.

*OR:*

The **OR** operator is used to combine two or more conditions, and the result is true if at least one of the conditions is true.

**Example**:

```
SELECT Name FROM Employees
WHERE Department = 'HR' OR Department = 'IT';
```

**Explanation**: This query retrieves employees who are in either the **HR** or **IT** department.

*NOT:*

The **NOT** operator negates a condition. The result is true if the condition is false.

**Example**:

```
SELECT Name FROM Employees
WHERE NOT Department = 'HR';
```

**Explanation**: This query retrieves employees who are not in the **HR** department.

---

## 5. Arithmetic Operators

Arithmetic operators perform mathematical operations on numeric values. These are commonly used for calculations like sums, differences, products, and quotients.

*Addition (+):*

The + operator adds two numbers together.

**Example**:

```
SELECT Salary + 5000 AS New_Salary FROM Employees;
```

**Explanation**: This query adds 5,000 to the **Salary** of each employee.

*Subtraction (-):*

The - operator subtracts one number from another.

**Example**:

```
SELECT Salary - 2000 AS Reduced_Salary FROM Employees;
```

**Explanation**: This query subtracts 2,000 from the **Salary** of each employee.

*Multiplication (*):*

The * operator multiplies two numbers together.

**Example**:

```
SELECT Salary * 1.10 AS Increased_Salary FROM Employees;
```

**Explanation**: This query increases the **Salary** by 10% by multiplying it by **1.10**.

*Division (/):*

The / operator divides one number by another.

**Example**:

```
SELECT Salary / 12 AS Monthly_Salary FROM Employees;
```

**Explanation**: This query calculates the monthly salary by dividing the **Salary** by 12.

---

## Summary Table

| Function Type | Function | Description | Example Query |
|---|---|---|---|
| **Aggregate Functions** | SUM() | Calculates the total sum of a numeric column. | `SELECT SUM(Salary) FROM Employees;` |
| | AVG() | Calculates the average of a numeric column. | `SELECT AVG(Salary) FROM Employees;` |
| | COUNT() | Counts the number of rows or entries. | `SELECT COUNT(*) FROM Employees;` |
| | MIN() | Finds the minimum value in a column. | `SELECT MIN(Salary) FROM Employees;` |
| | MAX() | Finds the maximum value in a column. | `SELECT MAX(Salary) FROM Employees;` |
| **String Functions** | CONCAT() | Concatenates two or more strings. | `SELECT CONCAT(FirstName, ' ', LastName) FROM Employees;` |
| | SUBSTRING() | Extracts a substring from a string. | `SELECT SUBSTRING(Name, 1, 3) FROM Employees;` |
| | LENGTH() | Returns the length of a string. | `SELECT LENGTH(Name) FROM Employees;` |
| **Date & Time Functions** | NOW() | Returns the current date and time. | `SELECT NOW();` |
| | DATE_ADD() | Adds a specified interval to a date. | `SELECT DATE_ADD(HireDate, INTERVAL 1 YEAR) FROM Employees;` |
| | DATE_DIFF() | Calculates the difference between two dates. | `SELECT DATEDIFF(CURRENT_DATE, HireDate) FROM Employees;` |

| Function Type | Function | Description | Example Query |
|---|---|---|---|
| **Logical Operators** | AND | Combines two conditions, true only if both are true. | `SELECT Name FROM Employees WHERE Department = 'HR' AND Salary > 50000;` |
| | OR | Combines two conditions, true if either one is true. | `SELECT Name FROM Employees WHERE Department = 'HR' OR Department = 'IT';` |
| | NOT | Negates a condition, true if the condition is false. | `SELECT Name FROM Employees WHERE NOT Department = 'HR';` |
| **Arithmetic Operators** | + | Adds two numbers. | `SELECT Salary + 5000 FROM Employees;` |
| | - | Subtracts one number from another. | `SELECT Salary - 2000 FROM Employees;` |
| | * | Multiplies two numbers. | `SELECT Salary * 1.10 FROM Employees;` |
| | / | Divides one number by another. | `SELECT Salary / 12 FROM Employees;` |

These functions and operators are crucial for performing advanced data manipulations and calculations within SQL queries, making them a powerful tool for data analysts and database administrators.

## 1. Aggregate Functions

### *1.1 SUM() - Total Salary*

The **SUM()** function calculates the total of a numeric column, such as the total salary of employees.

```
SELECT SUM(Salary) AS TotalSalary FROM Employees;
```

**Explanation**: This query sums all the salaries in the **Employees** table.

---

### *1.2 AVG() - Average Salary*

The **AVG()** function calculates the average of a numeric column, such as the average salary of employees.

```
SELECT AVG(Salary) AS AverageSalary FROM Employees;
```

**Explanation**: This query calculates the average salary of all employees in the **Employees** table.

---

*1.3 COUNT() - Employee Count*

The **COUNT()** function counts the number of rows in a table or the number of rows that satisfy a specific condition.

```
SELECT COUNT(*) AS EmployeeCount FROM Employees;
```

**Explanation**: This query returns the total number of employees in the **Employees** table.

---

*1.4 MIN() - Minimum Salary*

The **MIN()** function returns the smallest value in a column.

```
SELECT MIN(Salary) AS MinSalary FROM Employees;
```

**Explanation**: This query returns the lowest salary in the **Employees** table.

---

*1.5 MAX() - Maximum Salary*

The **MAX()** function returns the largest value in a column.

```
SELECT MAX(Salary) AS MaxSalary FROM Employees;
```

**Explanation**: This query returns the highest salary in the **Employees** table.

---

## 2. String Functions

*2.1 CONCAT() - Concatenate First and Last Name*

The **CONCAT()** function joins two or more strings together.

```
SELECT CONCAT(FirstName, ' ', LastName) AS FullName FROM Employees;
```

**Explanation**: This query concatenates the **FirstName** and **LastName** columns to create a **FullName** column.

*2.2 SUBSTRING() - Extract Part of Email*

The **SUBSTRING()** function extracts a portion of a string.

```
SELECT SUBSTRING(Email, 1, 5) AS ShortEmail FROM Employees;
```

**Explanation**: This query extracts the first 5 characters from the **Email** column.

---

*2.3 LENGTH() - Length of Name*

The **LENGTH()** function returns the number of characters in a string.

```
SELECT LENGTH(Name) AS NameLength FROM Employees;
```

**Explanation**: This query returns the length of the **Name** column for each employee.

---

## 3. Date and Time Functions

*3.1 NOW() - Current Date and Time*

The **NOW()** function returns the current date and time.

```
SELECT NOW() AS CurrentDateTime;
```

**Explanation**: This query returns the current date and time.

---

*3.2 DATE_ADD() - Add One Year to Hire Date*

The **DATE_ADD()** function adds a specified time interval to a date.

```
SELECT DATE_ADD(HireDate, INTERVAL 1 YEAR) AS OneYearLater FROM Employees;
```

**Explanation**: This query adds one year to the **HireDate** of each employee.

---

*3.3 DATE_DIFF() - Days Employed*

The **DATE_DIFF()** function calculates the difference between two dates.

```
SELECT DATEDIFF(CURRENT_DATE, HireDate) AS DaysEmployed FROM Employees;
```

**Explanation**: This query calculates how many days each employee has been employed by subtracting **HireDate** from the current date.

---

## 4. Logical Operators

### *4.1 AND - Multiple Conditions*

The **AND** operator is used to combine two or more conditions. It returns true if all conditions are true.

```
SELECT Name FROM Employees WHERE Department = 'HR' AND Salary > 50000;
```

**Explanation**: This query retrieves the names of employees in the **HR** department with a salary greater than 50,000.

---

### *4.2 OR - Either Condition*

The **OR** operator is used to combine conditions. It returns true if at least one condition is true.

```
SELECT Name FROM Employees WHERE Department = 'HR' OR Department = 'IT';
```

**Explanation**: This query retrieves employees who are either in the **HR** or **IT** department.

---

### *4.3 NOT - Exclude a Department*

The **NOT** operator negates a condition. It returns true if the condition is false.

```
SELECT Name FROM Employees WHERE NOT Department = 'HR';
```

**Explanation**: This query retrieves the names of employees who are **not** in the **HR** department.

---

## 5. Arithmetic Operators

### *5.1 + (Addition) - Increase Salary*

The + operator adds two numbers together.

```
SELECT Salary + 5000 AS IncreasedSalary FROM Employees;
```

**Explanation**: This query increases the **Salary** by 5,000 for each employee.

---

### *5.2 - (Subtraction) - Deduct Salary*

The **-** operator subtracts one number from another.

```
SELECT Salary - 2000 AS ReducedSalary FROM Employees;
```

**Explanation**: This query subtracts 2,000 from the **Salary** of each employee.

---

### *5.3 * (Multiplication) - Increase Salary by 10%*

The * operator multiplies two numbers.

```
SELECT Salary * 1.10 AS IncreasedSalary FROM Employees;
```

**Explanation**: This query increases the **Salary** by 10% for each employee.

---

### *5.4 / (Division) - Monthly Salary*

The / operator divides one number by another.

```
SELECT Salary / 12 AS MonthlySalary FROM Employees;
```

**Explanation**: This query divides the **Salary** by 12 to calculate the monthly salary of each employee.

---

### *5.5 Modulus (%) - Find Remainder of Salary Division*

The **%** operator returns the remainder of division.

```
SELECT Salary % 1000 AS SalaryRemainder FROM Employees;
```

**Explanation**: This query returns the remainder when the **Salary** is divided by 1,000.

---

## 6. Practical Examples with Graphical Diagrams

Let's break down the following practical SQL example using a simple graphical diagram.

### 6.1 Example: SUM() and COUNT()

We will use the **SUM()** and **COUNT()** functions to calculate the total salary and the number of employees.

**Query**:

```
SELECT SUM(Salary) AS TotalSalary, COUNT(*) AS EmployeeCount FROM Employees;
```

**Explanation**:

- The **SUM(Salary)** function sums all the salary values.
- The **COUNT(*)** function counts the number of employees.

**Graphical Representation**:

| Employee Name | Salary |
|---|---|
| John | 50000 |
| Jane | 60000 |
| Bob | 55000 |
| Alice | 70000 |

- **Total Salary** = 50000 + 60000 + 55000 + 70000 = **245000**
- **Employee Count** = 4

---

### 6.2 Example: CONCAT()

Let's concatenate the first and last name to create a full name.

**Query**:

```
SELECT CONCAT(FirstName, ' ', LastName) AS FullName FROM Employees;
```

**Graphical Representation**:

| FirstName | LastName | FullName |
|---|---|---|
| John | Doe | John Doe |
| Jane | Smith | Jane Smith |

---

### *6.3 Example: DATE_ADD()*

We'll add one year to each employee's hire date.

**Query**:

```
SELECT Name, DATE_ADD(HireDate, INTERVAL 1 YEAR) AS NextAnniversary FROM
Employees;
```

**Graphical Representation**:

| Name | HireDate | NextAnniversary |
|---|---|---|
| John | 2015-06-15 | 2016-06-15 |
| Jane | 2016-07-20 | 2017-07-20 |

---

### *6.4 Example: Logical Operator (AND)*

We'll select employees from the **HR** department with a salary greater than 50,000.

**Query**:

```
SELECT Name FROM Employees WHERE Department = 'HR' AND Salary > 50000;
```

**Graphical Representation**:

| Name | Department | Salary |
|---|---|---|
| Alice | HR | 60000 |

## CHAPTER-5

# Working with Joins and Subqueries

In SQL, **joins** and **subqueries** are used to combine data from multiple tables or queries. Below is a detailed explanation of joins and subqueries, along with their types and examples.

---

## 1. Understanding Joins: INNER, OUTER, LEFT, RIGHT, CROSS

**Joins** are used to combine rows from two or more tables based on a related column between them. SQL provides different types of joins, each serving a different purpose.

---

### *1.1 INNER JOIN*

An **INNER JOIN** returns only the rows where there is a match in both tables.

**Syntax:**

```
SELECT columns
FROM table1
INNER JOIN table2
ON table1.column = table2.column;
```

**Example:**

```
SELECT Employees.Name, Departments.DepartmentName
FROM Employees
INNER JOIN Departments
ON Employees.DepartmentID = Departments.DepartmentID;
```

**Explanation:**

- This query returns only the employees who belong to a department. If an employee doesn't have a matching department, they won't be included in the result.

**Result:**

| Name | DepartmentName |
|---|---|
| John | IT |
| Alice | HR |

---

### *1.2 LEFT JOIN (or LEFT OUTER JOIN)*

A **LEFT JOIN** returns all rows from the **left table**, and the matched rows from the **right table**. If no match is found, **NULL** values are returned for columns from the **right table**.

**Syntax:**

```
SELECT columns
FROM table1
LEFT JOIN table2
ON table1.column = table2.column;
```

**Example:**

```
SELECT Employees.Name, Departments.DepartmentName
FROM Employees
LEFT JOIN Departments
ON Employees.DepartmentID = Departments.DepartmentID;
```

**Explanation:**

- This query returns all employees, including those who don't belong to any department. If an employee doesn't belong to any department, the department field will be **NULL**.

**Result:**

| Name | DepartmentName |
|---|---|
| John | IT |
| Alice | HR |
| Bob | NULL |

---

### *1.3 RIGHT JOIN (or RIGHT OUTER JOIN)*

A **RIGHT JOIN** returns all rows from the **right table**, and the matched rows from the **left table**. If no match is found, **NULL** values are returned for columns from the **left table**.

**Syntax:**

```
SELECT columns
FROM table1
RIGHT JOIN table2
ON table1.column = table2.column;
```

**Example:**

```
SELECT Employees.Name, Departments.DepartmentName
FROM Employees
RIGHT JOIN Departments
ON Employees.DepartmentID = Departments.DepartmentID;
```

**Explanation:**

- This query returns all departments, including those with no employees. If a department has no employees, the employee field will be **NULL**.

**Result:**

| Name | DepartmentName |
|---|---|
| John | IT |
| Alice | HR |
| NULL | Finance |

---

### *1.4 FULL OUTER JOIN*

A **FULL OUTER JOIN** returns all rows from both tables. If there is no match, **NULL** values are returned for missing matches from either side.

**Syntax:**

```
SELECT columns
FROM table1
FULL OUTER JOIN table2
ON table1.column = table2.column;
```

**Example:**

```
SELECT Employees.Name, Departments.DepartmentName
FROM Employees
FULL OUTER JOIN Departments
ON Employees.DepartmentID = Departments.DepartmentID;
```

**Explanation:**

- This query returns all employees and all departments, with **NULL** values where there are no matching records.

**Result:**

| Name | DepartmentName |
| --- | --- |
| John | IT |
| Alice | HR |
| Bob | NULL |
| NULL | Finance |

---

*1.5 CROSS JOIN*

A **CROSS JOIN** returns the Cartesian product of both tables. This means that it combines every row from the first table with every row from the second table.

**Syntax:**

```
SELECT columns
FROM table1
CROSS JOIN table2;
```

**Example:**

```
SELECT Employees.Name, Departments.DepartmentName
FROM Employees
CROSS JOIN Departments;
```

**Explanation:**

- This query returns a combination of every employee with every department, resulting in all possible pairings.

**Result:**

| Name | DepartmentName |
| --- | --- |
| John | HR |
| John | IT |
| John | Finance |

**Name DepartmentName**

Alice HR

Alice IT

Alice Finance

---

## 2. Using Self-Joins

A **self-join** is a join where a table is joined with itself. This is typically used when we need to compare rows within the same table.

### Example:

```
SELECT E1.Name AS EmployeeName, E2.Name AS ManagerName
FROM Employees E1
JOIN Employees E2
ON E1.ManagerID = E2.EmployeeID;
```

### Explanation:

- This query retrieves the names of employees along with their managers (assuming each employee has a **ManagerID** that corresponds to an **EmployeeID**).

---

## 3. Writing Subqueries in SELECT, FROM, and WHERE

A **subquery** is a query within another query. Subqueries are used to retrieve data that will be used in the main query.

---

### *3.1 Subqueries in SELECT*

A subquery can be used in the **SELECT** statement to return a value for each row.

### Example:

```
SELECT Name, (SELECT DepartmentName FROM Departments WHERE DepartmentID =
Employees.DepartmentID) AS Department
FROM Employees;
```

**Explanation:**

- This query retrieves the **Name** of each employee and the corresponding **DepartmentName** using a subquery.

---

### *3.2 Subqueries in FROM*

A subquery can also be used in the **FROM** clause, where the result of the subquery is treated as a temporary table.

**Example:**

```
SELECT Temp.Name, Temp.Salary
FROM (SELECT Name, Salary FROM Employees WHERE Salary > 50000) AS Temp;
```

**Explanation:**

- The subquery returns employees with a salary greater than 50,000, and the outer query selects the **Name** and **Salary** from this temporary result set.

---

### *3.3 Subqueries in WHERE*

Subqueries are often used in the **WHERE** clause to filter results based on conditions.

**Example:**

```
SELECT Name
FROM Employees
WHERE DepartmentID = (SELECT DepartmentID FROM Departments WHERE
DepartmentName = 'HR');
```

**Explanation:**

- This query retrieves the names of employees who belong to the **HR** department.

---

## 4. Correlated vs. Non-Correlated Subqueries

---

### *4.1 Correlated Subquery*

A **correlated subquery** refers to a subquery that depends on the outer query. It is evaluated once for each row processed by the outer query.

**Example:**

```
SELECT Name
FROM Employees E1
WHERE Salary > (SELECT AVG(Salary) FROM Employees E2 WHERE E2.DepartmentID =
E1.DepartmentID);
```

**Explanation:**

- This query selects employees whose salary is greater than the average salary in their department. The subquery refers to the outer query's **DepartmentID**.

---

### 4.2 Non-Correlated Subquery

A **non-correlated subquery** does not depend on the outer query. It is executed once and the result is used by the outer query.

**Example:**

```
SELECT Name
FROM Employees
WHERE DepartmentID = (SELECT DepartmentID FROM Departments WHERE
DepartmentName = 'IT');
```

**Explanation:**

- This query selects employees who work in the **IT** department, and the subquery returns the department ID for **IT**.

---

## 5. Combining Data with UNION and INTERSECT

---

### 5.1 UNION

The **UNION** operator is used to combine the results of two or more queries into a single result set. It removes duplicate records.

**Syntax:**

```
SELECT column1, column2 FROM table1
UNION
SELECT column1, column2 FROM table2;
```

**Example:**

```
SELECT Name FROM Employees
UNION
SELECT Name FROM Contractors;
```

**Explanation:**

- This query combines the names of all employees and contractors, removing duplicates.

---

### *5.2 INTERSECT*

The **INTERSECT** operator returns the common rows from two queries.

**Syntax:**

```
SELECT column1, column2 FROM table1
INTERSECT
SELECT column1, column2 FROM table2;
```

**Example:**

```
SELECT Name FROM Employees
INTERSECT
SELECT Name FROM Contractors;
```

**Explanation:**

- This query returns the names of individuals who are both employees and contractors.

---

## 1. INNER JOIN Example: Employees and Departments

**Scenario:** Retrieve employees and their department names.

```
SELECT Employees.Name, Departments.DepartmentName
FROM Employees
INNER JOIN Departments
ON Employees.DepartmentID = Departments.DepartmentID;
```

**Result:**

| Name | DepartmentName |
|---|---|
| John | HR |
| Alice | IT |

| Name | DepartmentName |
| --- | --- |
| Bob | Finance |

---

## 2. LEFT JOIN Example: Employees and Departments

**Scenario:** Retrieve all employees and their departments (if any).

```
SELECT Employees.Name, Departments.DepartmentName
FROM Employees
LEFT JOIN Departments
ON Employees.DepartmentID = Departments.DepartmentID;
```

**Result:**

| Name | DepartmentName |
| --- | --- |
| John | HR |
| Alice | IT |
| Bob | NULL |

---

## 3. RIGHT JOIN Example: Departments and Employees

**Scenario:** Retrieve all departments and the employees working in them (if any).

```
SELECT Employees.Name, Departments.DepartmentName
FROM Employees
RIGHT JOIN Departments
ON Employees.DepartmentID = Departments.DepartmentID;
```

**Result:**

| Name | DepartmentName |
| --- | --- |
| John | HR |
| Alice | IT |
| NULL | Finance |

---

## 4. FULL OUTER JOIN Example: Employees and Departments

**Scenario:** Retrieve all employees and all departments, including unmatched records.

```
SELECT Employees.Name, Departments.DepartmentName
```

```
FROM Employees
FULL OUTER JOIN Departments
ON Employees.DepartmentID = Departments.DepartmentID;
```

**Result:**

| Name | DepartmentName |
|---|---|
| John | HR |
| Alice | IT |
| Bob | NULL |
| NULL | Finance |

---

## 5. CROSS JOIN Example: Employees and Departments

**Scenario:** Generate all possible combinations of employees and departments.

```
SELECT Employees.Name, Departments.DepartmentName
FROM Employees
CROSS JOIN Departments;
```

**Result:**

| Name | DepartmentName |
|---|---|
| John | HR |
| John | IT |
| John | Finance |
| Alice | HR |
| Alice | IT |
| Alice | Finance |

---

## 6. Self JOIN Example: Employees with Managers

**Scenario:** Retrieve employee names along with their manager's name.

```
SELECT E1.Name AS EmployeeName, E2.Name AS ManagerName
FROM Employees E1
JOIN Employees E2
ON E1.ManagerID = E2.EmployeeID;
```

**Result:**

| EmployeeName | ManagerName |
|---|---|
| John | Alice |
| Bob | Alice |

---

## 7. Subquery in SELECT: Department Salary Average

**Scenario:** Retrieve employees and the average salary of their departments.

```
SELECT Name,
       (SELECT AVG(Salary) FROM Employees E2 WHERE E2.DepartmentID =
E1.DepartmentID) AS AvgSalary
FROM Employees E1;
```

**Result:**

| Name | AvgSalary |
|---|---|
| John | 55000 |
| Alice | 60000 |
| Bob | 50000 |

---

## 8. Subquery in FROM: Subquery as a Table

**Scenario:** Retrieve the average salary for each department.

```
SELECT DepartmentID, AVG(Salary) AS AvgSalary
FROM (SELECT DepartmentID, Salary FROM Employees) AS SubQuery
GROUP BY DepartmentID;
```

**Result:**

| DepartmentID | AvgSalary |
|---|---|
| 1 | 60000 |
| 2 | 55000 |

---

## 9. Subquery in WHERE: Employees with Higher Salary than Average

**Scenario:** Retrieve employees whose salary is higher than the average salary in their department.

```
SELECT Name
FROM Employees E1
```

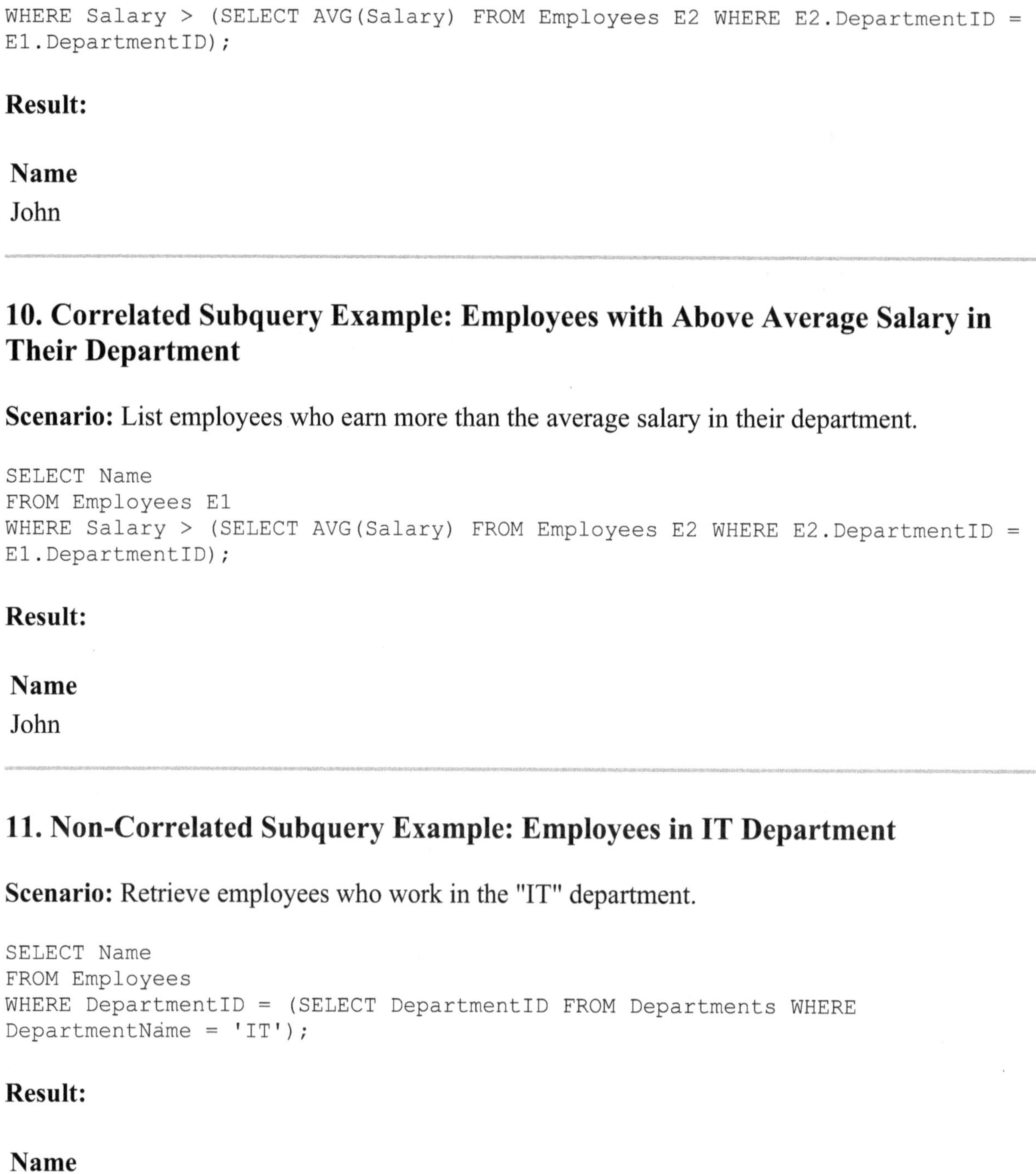

```
WHERE Salary > (SELECT AVG(Salary) FROM Employees E2 WHERE E2.DepartmentID =
E1.DepartmentID);
```

**Result:**

| Name |
|---|
| John |

---

## 10. Correlated Subquery Example: Employees with Above Average Salary in Their Department

**Scenario:** List employees who earn more than the average salary in their department.

```
SELECT Name
FROM Employees E1
WHERE Salary > (SELECT AVG(Salary) FROM Employees E2 WHERE E2.DepartmentID =
E1.DepartmentID);
```

**Result:**

| Name |
|---|
| John |

---

## 11. Non-Correlated Subquery Example: Employees in IT Department

**Scenario:** Retrieve employees who work in the "IT" department.

```
SELECT Name
FROM Employees
WHERE DepartmentID = (SELECT DepartmentID FROM Departments WHERE
DepartmentName = 'IT');
```

**Result:**

| Name |
|---|
| Alice |

---

## 12. Combining Data with UNION: Employees and Contractors

**Scenario:** Combine the names of employees and contractors into one result set.

```
SELECT Name FROM Employees
UNION
```

```
SELECT Name FROM Contractors;
```

**Result:**

| Name |
|---|
| John |
| Alice |
| Bob |

---

## 13. Combining Data with UNION ALL: Employees and Contractors

**Scenario:** Combine the names of employees and contractors, including duplicates.

```
SELECT Name FROM Employees
UNION ALL
SELECT Name FROM Contractors;
```

**Result:**

| Name |
|---|
| John |
| Alice |
| Bob |
| John |

---

## 14. Combining Data with INTERSECT: Common Employees

**Scenario:** Retrieve names of people who are both employees and contractors.

```
SELECT Name FROM Employees
INTERSECT
SELECT Name FROM Contractors;
```

**Result:**

| Name |
|---|
| John |

---

## 15. INNER JOIN with Multiple Conditions

**Scenario:** Retrieve employees with salary greater than 50,000 and their department names.

```
SELECT Employees.Name, Departments.DepartmentName
FROM Employees
INNER JOIN Departments
ON Employees.DepartmentID = Departments.DepartmentID
WHERE Employees.Salary > 50000;
```

**Result:**

| Name | DepartmentName |
|---|---|
| Alice | IT |

---

## 16. LEFT JOIN with NULL Condition

**Scenario:** Retrieve all employees and their departments, including those who don't belong to any department.

```
SELECT Employees.Name, Departments.DepartmentName
FROM Employees
LEFT JOIN Departments
ON Employees.DepartmentID = Departments.DepartmentID
WHERE Departments.DepartmentName IS NULL;
```

**Result:**

| Name | DepartmentName |
|---|---|
| Bob | NULL |

---

## 17. RIGHT JOIN with NULL Condition

**Scenario:** Retrieve all departments and their employees, including those without employees.

```
SELECT Employees.Name, Departments.DepartmentName
FROM Employees
RIGHT JOIN Departments
ON Employees.DepartmentID = Departments.DepartmentID
WHERE Employees.Name IS NULL;
```

**Result:**

| Name | DepartmentName |
|---|---|
| NULL | Finance |

---

## 18. Using Subquery in HAVING Clause

**Scenario:** Retrieve departments with an average salary greater than 50,000.

```
SELECT DepartmentID, AVG(Salary) AS AvgSalary
FROM Employees
GROUP BY DepartmentID
HAVING AVG(Salary) > (SELECT AVG(Salary) FROM Employees);
```

**Result:**

| DepartmentID | AvgSalary |
|---|---|
| 1 | 60000 |

---

## 19. Combining Data with UNION and ORDER BY

**Scenario:** Combine employees from two departments and order by name.

```
SELECT Name FROM Employees WHERE DepartmentID = 1
UNION
SELECT Name FROM Employees WHERE DepartmentID = 2
ORDER BY Name;
```

**Result:**

| Name |
|---|
| Alice |
| Bob |
| John |

---

## 20. Subquery in UPDATE: Updating Employee Salary Based on Department Average

**Scenario:** Increase salary of employees whose salary is lower than the department average.

```
UPDATE Employees
SET Salary = Salary * 1.1
WHERE Salary < (SELECT AVG(Salary) FROM Employees WHERE DepartmentID = 1);
```

## Conclusion

**Joins** and **subqueries** are essential for combining and filtering data in relational databases. Understanding how to use **INNER JOIN**, **LEFT JOIN**, **RIGHT JOIN**, **FULL OUTER JOIN**, and **CROSS JOIN** allows you to retrieve and manipulate data from multiple tables. Additionally, subqueries, whether correlated or non-correlated, are powerful tools for filtering and processing data. Combining data with **UNION** and **INTERSECT** enables advanced data aggregation and retrieval techniques.

# CHAPTER-6

# ADVANCED QUERY TECHNIQUES

Advanced query techniques in SQL are used to perform complex data retrieval and manipulation tasks. These techniques involve advanced concepts and can be very powerful when querying large or intricate databases. Below are detailed explanations of key advanced query techniques:

---

### *1. Using CASE Statements*

The `CASE` statement in SQL is a conditional expression that allows you to perform different actions based on specific conditions. It works like an IF-THEN-ELSE statement in other programming languages.

Syntax of CASE:

```
SELECT column1,
       column2,
       CASE
           WHEN condition1 THEN result1
           WHEN condition2 THEN result2
           ELSE result3
       END AS new_column
FROM table_name;
```

Example:

```
SELECT Name,
       Salary,
       CASE
           WHEN Salary > 50000 THEN 'High Salary'
           WHEN Salary BETWEEN 30000 AND 50000 THEN 'Medium Salary'
           ELSE 'Low Salary'
       END AS Salary_Category
FROM Employees;
```

**Explanation:**

- This query classifies employees based on their salary into 'High Salary', 'Medium Salary', or 'Low Salary' categories.
- The `CASE` statement evaluates each condition for every row and returns the corresponding result.

---

### *2. Window Functions (ROW_NUMBER, RANK, PARTITION BY)*

Window functions allow you to perform calculations across a set of table rows that are related to the current row. These functions are used with the `OVER` clause and can provide insights like ranking, running totals, and partitioned analysis.

Common Window Functions:

- `ROW_NUMBER()`: Assigns a unique sequential number to rows within a partition of a result set.
- `RANK()`: Assigns a rank to each row, with gaps in ranking for tied values.
- `PARTITION BY`: Divides the result set into partitions and applies the window function to each partition.

Syntax of Window Function:

```
SELECT column1,
       column2,
       ROW_NUMBER() OVER (PARTITION BY column1 ORDER BY column2) AS row_num
FROM table_name;
```

Example:

```
SELECT Name,
       Salary,
       ROW_NUMBER() OVER (PARTITION BY Department ORDER BY Salary DESC) AS
RowNum
FROM Employees;
```

## Explanation:

- This query ranks employees by salary within each department.
- The `PARTITION BY` clause divides the data into separate departments, and `ROW_NUMBER()` assigns a unique number to each employee within their department, ordered by salary in descending order.

---

*3. Recursive Queries with CTEs (Common Table Expressions)*

A recursive query allows you to perform operations that require referencing the result of a previous query or result set. This is typically used for hierarchical or tree-structured data, like organizational charts.

Syntax of Recursive CTE:

```
WITH RECURSIVE CTE_Name AS (
    -- Base case: select the starting point
    SELECT column1, column2
    FROM table_name
    WHERE condition
    UNION ALL
    -- Recursive case: select related data
    SELECT column1, column2
    FROM table_name
    JOIN CTE_Name ON table_name.column1 = CTE_Name.column1
)
SELECT * FROM CTE_Name;
```

Example:

```
WITH RECURSIVE OrgChart AS (
    -- Base case: select the CEO
    SELECT EmployeeID, ManagerID, Name
```

```
    FROM Employees
    WHERE ManagerID IS NULL
    UNION ALL
    -- Recursive case: select employees reporting to the manager
    SELECT e.EmployeeID, e.ManagerID, e.Name
    FROM Employees e
    JOIN OrgChart o ON e.ManagerID = o.EmployeeID
)
SELECT * FROM OrgChart;
```

**Explanation:**

- This query generates an organizational chart starting from the CEO and recursively fetching all employees reporting to managers.
- The recursive CTE allows you to traverse through hierarchical relationships within the data.

---

### 4. Pivoting and Unpivoting Data

Pivoting and unpivoting are techniques to transform rows into columns and vice versa, helping to reorganize data for better analysis and reporting.

#### Pivoting:

Pivoting converts rows into columns. SQL Server and other databases support the `PIVOT` operator to achieve this.

Syntax of PIVOT:

```
SELECT column1, [value1], [value2], [value3]
FROM
  (SELECT column1, column2, value_column
   FROM table_name) AS SourceTable
PIVOT
  (SUM(value_column)
   FOR column2 IN ([value1], [value2], [value3])) AS PivotTable;
```

Example (Pivot):

```
SELECT Department,
       [2022], [2023]
FROM
  (SELECT Department, Year, Revenue
   FROM RevenueData) AS SourceTable
PIVOT
  (SUM(Revenue) FOR Year IN ([2022], [2023])) AS PivotTable;
```

**Explanation:**

- This query converts rows showing revenue data for different years into separate columns for each year.
- The `PIVOT` operator allows data for each department to be displayed as columns (2022, 2023) instead of rows.

### Unpivoting:

Unpivoting is the reverse operation of pivoting, transforming columns into rows.

#### Syntax of UNPIVOT:

```
SELECT column1, column2, value_column
FROM
   (SELECT column1, [value1], [value2], [value3]
    FROM table_name) AS SourceTable
UNPIVOT
   (value_column FOR column2 IN ([value1], [value2], [value3])) AS
UnpivotTable;
```

#### Example (Unpivot):

```
SELECT Department, Year, Revenue
FROM
   (SELECT Department, [2022], [2023]
    FROM RevenueData) AS SourceTable
UNPIVOT
   (Revenue FOR Year IN ([2022], [2023])) AS UnpivotTable;
```

**Explanation:**

- This query converts columns for different years into rows, making it easier to perform time-based analysis.

---

## *5. Advanced Filtering Techniques*

Advanced filtering in SQL allows you to apply complex conditions to retrieve specific data. These techniques include the use of subqueries, pattern matching, and logical operators.

### Using IN, LIKE, and BETWEEN:

- **IN**: Allows you to specify multiple possible values for a column.
- **LIKE**: Used for pattern matching with wildcards (`%` for any sequence of characters, _ for a single character).
- **BETWEEN**: Filters records within a specific range.

#### Example:

```
SELECT Name, Department, Salary
FROM Employees
WHERE Department IN ('HR', 'IT') AND Salary BETWEEN 30000 AND 60000;
```

**Explanation:**

- This query filters employees who belong to either the HR or IT departments and whose salaries fall between 30,000 and 60,000.

Using Regular Expressions (if supported):

Some databases support regular expressions for more complex pattern matching.

```
SELECT Name
FROM Employees
WHERE Name REGEXP '^J.*' -- Matches names starting with 'J'
```

Example using Subqueries for Filtering:

```
SELECT Name, Salary
FROM Employees
WHERE Department = (SELECT Department FROM Departments WHERE DepartmentID =
2);
```

**Explanation:**

- This query retrieves employees working in the department with ID 2 by using a subquery in the `WHERE` clause.

---

## 1. Using CASE Statements

*Example:*

Classifying employees based on their performance rating.

```
SELECT Name,
       Performance_Rating,
       CASE
           WHEN Performance_Rating >= 90 THEN 'Excellent'
           WHEN Performance_Rating BETWEEN 70 AND 89 THEN 'Good'
           WHEN Performance_Rating BETWEEN 50 AND 69 THEN 'Average'
           ELSE 'Poor'
       END AS Performance_Category
FROM Employees;
```

**Explanation:**

- This query classifies employees based on their `Performance_Rating` into categories: 'Excellent', 'Good', 'Average', or 'Poor'.

*Graphical Diagram:*

| Name | Performance_Rating | Performance_Category |
|---|---|---|
| John | 95 | Excellent |
| Sarah | 82 | Good |
| Alex | 55 | Average |
| Jennifer | 45 | Poor |

---

## 2. Window Functions (ROW_NUMBER, RANK, PARTITION BY)

*Example:*

Ranking employees within each department by salary.

```
SELECT Name, Department, Salary,
       ROW_NUMBER() OVER (PARTITION BY Department ORDER BY Salary DESC) AS
RowNum
FROM Employees;
```

### Explanation:

- The `ROW_NUMBER` function assigns a unique number to employees based on their salary within each department.

*Graphical Diagram:*

| Name | Department | Salary | RowNum |
|---|---|---|---|
| John | IT | 90000 | 1 |
| Sarah | IT | 85000 | 2 |
| Alex | HR | 80000 | 1 |
| Jennifer | HR | 75000 | 2 |

---

## 3. Recursive Queries with CTEs

*Example:*

Display the organizational hierarchy of employees.

```
WITH RECURSIVE OrgChart AS (
    SELECT EmployeeID, ManagerID, Name
    FROM Employees
    WHERE ManagerID IS NULL
    UNION ALL
    SELECT e.EmployeeID, e.ManagerID, e.Name
    FROM Employees e
    JOIN OrgChart o ON e.ManagerID = o.EmployeeID
)
SELECT * FROM OrgChart;
```

**Explanation:**

- This query uses a recursive CTE to display employees in an organizational hierarchy, starting from the top-level manager.

*Graphical Diagram:*

```
CEO
 |
 Manager1 -- Manager2
 |            |
 Employee1  Employee2
```

---

## 4. Pivoting Data

*Example:*

Transforming monthly sales data into separate columns for each month.

```
SELECT Product, [January], [February], [March]
FROM
  (SELECT Product, Month, Sales
   FROM SalesData) AS SourceTable
PIVOT
  (SUM(Sales) FOR Month IN ([January], [February], [March])) AS PivotTable;
```

**Explanation:**

- This query converts rows for sales by month into columns, summarizing total sales for each product across different months.

*Graphical Diagram:*

| Product | January | February | March |
|---|---|---|---|
| Product A | 200 | 250 | 300 |
| Product B | 150 | 180 | 210 |

---

## 5. Unpivoting Data

*Example:*

Converting columns for sales in different months back into rows.

```
SELECT Product, Month, Sales
FROM
  (SELECT Product, [January], [February], [March]
   FROM SalesData) AS SourceTable
UNPIVOT
  (Sales FOR Month IN ([January], [February], [March])) AS UnpivotTable;
```

### Explanation:

- This query unpivots data to transform monthly sales columns back into rows, which can help analyze the data by month.

*Graphical Diagram:*

| Product | Month | Sales |
|---|---|---|
| Product A | January | 200 |
| Product A | February | 250 |
| Product A | March | 300 |
| Product B | January | 150 |
| Product B | February | 180 |
| Product B | March | 210 |

---

## 6. Advanced Filtering Techniques: Using IN

*Example:*

Filtering employees who belong to either the HR or IT department.

```
SELECT Name, Department, Salary
FROM Employees
WHERE Department IN ('HR', 'IT');
```

**Explanation:**

- This query filters employees who are in the HR or IT department.

*Graphical Diagram:*

| Name | Department | Salary |
|---|---|---|
| John | IT | 90000 |
| Sarah | HR | 85000 |

---

## 7. Advanced Filtering Techniques: Using LIKE

*Example:*

Finding employees whose names start with 'J'.

```
SELECT Name, Department
FROM Employees
WHERE Name LIKE 'J%';
```

**Explanation:**

- This query retrieves employees whose names start with 'J' (e.g., John, Jennifer).

*Graphical Diagram:*

| Name | Department |
|---|---|
| John | IT |
| Jennifer | HR |

---

## 8. Advanced Filtering Techniques: Using BETWEEN

*Example:*

Getting employees with salaries between 50,000 and 70,000.

```
SELECT Name, Salary
FROM Employees
WHERE Salary BETWEEN 50000 AND 70000;
```

**Explanation:**

- This query filters employees whose salaries are within the range of 50,000 to 70,000.

*Graphical Diagram:*

| Name | Salary |
|---|---|
| Sarah | 65000 |
| Alex | 58000 |

---

## 9. Using RANK with Window Functions

*Example:*

Ranking employees within each department by salary, with ties having the same rank.

```
SELECT Name, Department, Salary,
       RANK() OVER (PARTITION BY Department ORDER BY Salary DESC) AS Rank
FROM Employees;
```

**Explanation:**

- The `RANK()` function assigns a rank to each employee within their department based on salary, with ties receiving the same rank.

*Graphical Diagram:*

| Name | Department | Salary | Rank |
|---|---|---|---|
| John | IT | 90000 | 1 |
| Sarah | IT | 85000 | 2 |
| Alex | HR | 80000 | 1 |
| Jennifer | HR | 75000 | 2 |

---

## 10. Using a Self-Join

*Example:*

Finding employees who report to other employees in the same department.

```
SELECT e1.Name AS Employee, e2.Name AS Manager
```

```
FROM Employees e1
JOIN Employees e2 ON e1.ManagerID = e2.EmployeeID;
```

### Explanation:

- A self-join allows you to join the same table (Employees) to itself to find relationships, such as managers and their subordinates.

*Graphical Diagram:*

| Employee | Manager |
|---|---|
| John | Sarah |
| Alex | John |
| Jennifer | Sarah |

## Summary:

- **CASE Statements** are used for conditional logic.
- **Window Functions** like `ROW_NUMBER`, `RANK`, and `PARTITION BY` help in advanced analytics and ranking.
- **Recursive Queries with CTEs** are useful for hierarchical data like organizational charts.
- **Pivoting and Unpivoting** allow transformation of data, making it easier to analyze trends across multiple columns or rows.
- **Advanced Filtering** techniques give you powerful ways to filter and refine your data retrieval using operators like `IN`, `LIKE`, `BETWEEN`, and regular expressions.

These techniques allow for more complex, dynamic queries, making it easier to handle sophisticated data analysis tasks.

## CHAPTER-7

## DATA MANIPULATION IN SQL

Data Manipulation Language (DML) is a subset of SQL used for managing data stored in tables. It includes operations like **INSERT**, **UPDATE**, and **DELETE**, which allow you to add, modify, or remove data. Let's explore each with examples and graphical representations.

---

### 1. Inserting Data into Tables

The **INSERT** statement is used to add new rows of data to a table.

*Syntax:*

```
INSERT INTO table_name (column1, column2, ...) VALUES (value1, value2, ...);
```

*Example:*

Assume a table named `students`:

| StudentID | Name | Age | Grade |
|---|---|---|---|
| 1 | Alice | 21 | A |

**Query:**

```
INSERT INTO students (StudentID, Name, Age, Grade) VALUES (2, 'Bob', 22,
'B');
```

**Resulting Table:**

| StudentID | Name | Age | Grade |
|---|---|---|---|
| 1 | Alice | 21 | A |
| 2 | Bob | 22 | B |

**Graphical Representation:**

- An arrow indicates data flowing into the `students` table.

---

## 2. Bulk Insert Operations

Bulk insert allows inserting multiple rows simultaneously.

*Syntax:*

```
INSERT INTO table_name (column1, column2, ...) VALUES
(value1a, value2a, ...),
(value1b, value2b, ...),
...;
```

*Example:*

```
INSERT INTO students (StudentID, Name, Age, Grade) VALUES
(3, 'Charlie', 20, 'A'),
(4, 'Diana', 23, 'B');
```

### Resulting Table:

| StudentID | Name | Age | Grade |
|---|---|---|---|
| 1 | Alice | 21 | A |
| 2 | Bob | 22 | B |
| 3 | Charlie | 20 | A |
| 4 | Diana | 23 | B |

---

## 3. Updating Existing Records

The **UPDATE** statement modifies data in existing rows.

*Syntax:*

```
UPDATE table_name SET column1 = value1, column2 = value2 WHERE condition;
```

*Example:*

Change Bob's grade to `A`.

### Query:

```
UPDATE students SET Grade = 'A' WHERE Name = 'Bob';
```

**Resulting Table:**

| StudentID | Name | Age | Grade |
|---|---|---|---|
| 1 | Alice | 21 | A |
| 2 | Bob | 22 | A |
| 3 | Charlie | 20 | A |
| 4 | Diana | 23 | B |

**Graphical Representation:**

- A "pen" icon over Bob's grade column.

---

## 4. Deleting Records Safely

The **DELETE** statement removes rows based on a condition.

*Syntax:*

```
DELETE FROM table_name WHERE condition;
```

*Example:*

Remove the record of Charlie.

**Query:**

```
DELETE FROM students WHERE Name = 'Charlie';
```

**Resulting Table:**

| StudentID | Name | Age | Grade |
|---|---|---|---|
| 1 | Alice | 21 | A |
| 2 | Bob | 22 | A |
| 4 | Diana | 23 | B |

---

## 5. Handling Errors in Data Manipulation

Errors in data manipulation can occur due to:

- Violating constraints (e.g., primary key, foreign key, not null).
- Syntax errors in SQL queries.
- Inconsistent data types.

*Example:*

```
INSERT INTO students (StudentID, Name, Age, Grade) VALUES (2, 'Eve',
'twenty', 'C');
```

**Error:** `Age` expects an integer but received a string.

*Solutions:*

1. Validate data before inserting or updating.
2. Use **TRY-CATCH** for error handling in complex SQL operations.

## 1. Simple Insert Operation

### Query:

```
INSERT INTO students (StudentID, Name, Age, Grade) VALUES (5, 'Eve', 19,
'B');
```

### Output Table:

| StudentID | Name | Age | Grade |
|---|---|---|---|
| 1 | Alice | 21 | A |
| 2 | Bob | 22 | A |
| 4 | Diana | 23 | B |
| 5 | Eve | 19 | B |

---

## 2. Insert with Missing Columns

### Query:

```
INSERT INTO students (StudentID, Name) VALUES (6, 'Frank');
```

### Output Table (Assuming Age and Grade allow NULL):

| StudentID | Name | Age | Grade |
|---|---|---|---|
| 1 | Alice | 21 | A |

| StudentID | Name | Age | Grade |
|---|---|---|---|
| 2 | Bob | 22 | A |
| 4 | Diana | 23 | B |
| 5 | Eve | 19 | B |
| 6 | Frank | NULL | NULL |

---

## 3. Bulk Insert Operation

**Query:**

```
INSERT INTO students (StudentID, Name, Age, Grade) VALUES
(7, 'Grace', 20, 'A'),
(8, 'Hannah', 22, 'B');
```

**Output Table:**

| StudentID | Name | Age | Grade |
|---|---|---|---|
| ... | ... | ... | ... |
| 7 | Grace | 20 | A |
| 8 | Hannah | 22 | B |

---

## 4. Update a Single Record

**Query:**

```
UPDATE students SET Grade = 'A+' WHERE Name = 'Hannah';
```

**Output Table:**

| StudentID | Name | Age | Grade |
|---|---|---|---|
| ... | ... | ... | ... |
| 8 | Hannah | 22 | A+ |

---

## 5. Update Multiple Records

**Query:**

```
UPDATE students SET Grade = 'C' WHERE Age > 22;
```

**Output Table:**

| StudentID | Name | Age | Grade |
| --- | --- | --- | --- |
| 4 | Diana | 23 | C |

---

## 6. Conditional Update

**Query:**

```
UPDATE students SET Age = Age + 1 WHERE Grade = 'A';
```

**Output Table:**

| StudentID | Name | Age | Grade |
| --- | --- | --- | --- |
| 1 | Alice | 22 | A |
| 7 | Grace | 21 | A |

---

## 7. Safe Delete Operation

**Query:**

```
DELETE FROM students WHERE Name = 'Frank';
```

**Output Table:**

| StudentID | Name | Age | Grade |
| --- | --- | --- | --- |
| ... | ... | ... | ... |

---

## 8. Delete All Rows with Specific Grade

**Query:**

```
DELETE FROM students WHERE Grade = 'C';
```

**Output Table:**

| StudentID | Name | Age | Grade |
| --- | --- | --- | --- |
| ... | ... | ... | ... |

---

## 9. Handling Errors: Duplicate Key

**Query:**

```
INSERT INTO students (StudentID, Name, Age, Grade) VALUES (1, 'Alice', 21,
'A');
```

**Error:** `Duplicate entry '1' for key 'PRIMARY'`

---

## 10. Handling Errors: Data Type Mismatch

**Query:**

```
INSERT INTO students (StudentID, Name, Age, Grade) VALUES (9, 'Ian',
'twenty', 'B');
```

**Error:** `Incorrect integer value: 'twenty' for column 'Age'`

---

## 11. Insert Data Using Subquery

**Query:**

```
INSERT INTO students (StudentID, Name, Age, Grade)
SELECT 10, 'John', 25, 'A' FROM dual WHERE NOT EXISTS
(SELECT * FROM students WHERE Name = 'John');
```

**Output Table:**

| StudentID | Name | Age | Grade |
|---|---|---|---|
| ... | ... | ... | ... |
| 10 | John | 25 | A |

---

## 12. Update Based on Another Table

**Query:**

```
UPDATE students s
SET Grade = 'B+'
WHERE s.StudentID IN (SELECT StudentID FROM scholarship WHERE Amount > 5000);
```

**Output Table:**

- Rows updated based on matching StudentID from the `scholarship` table.

---

## 13. Insert with Default Values

**Query:**

```
INSERT INTO students (StudentID, Name) VALUES (11, 'Kate');
```

**Output Table:**

| StudentID | Name | Age | Grade |
|---|---|---|---|
| 11 | Kate | NULL | NULL |

---

## 14. Delete Without Affecting All Rows

**Query:**

```
DELETE FROM students WHERE Age IS NULL;
```

**Output Table:**

- Removes rows with missing `Age`.

---

## 15. Updating a Computed Column

**Query:**

```
UPDATE students SET Grade = CONCAT(Grade, '+') WHERE Grade IN ('A', 'B');
```

**Output Table:**

| StudentID | Name | Age | Grade |
|---|---|---|---|
| ... | ... | ... | A+ |
| ... | ... | ... | B+ |

# CHAPTER-8

## 1. PRINCIPLES OF DATABASE DESIGN

*Explanation*

Database design is the process of organizing data into a structured format that is efficient, easy to maintain, and scalable. The principles include:

- **Clarity:** Tables should represent a single entity or concept.
- **Consistency:** Data should not be redundant or ambiguous.
- **Scalability:** The design should handle future data growth.
- **Data Integrity:** Ensure relationships between tables are maintained using keys and constraints.

*Example:*

**Poor Design:** A single table storing employees and their department information.

| EmpID | Name | DeptName | DeptLocation |
|---|---|---|---|
| 1 | Alice | HR | New York |
| 2 | Bob | IT | San Francisco |

**Improved Design (Separation):**

1. **Employee Table:**

| EmpID | Name |
|---|---|
| 1 | Alice |
| 2 | Bob |

2. **Department Table:**

| DeptID | DeptName | DeptLocation |
|---|---|---|
| 1 | HR | New York |
| 2 | IT | San Francisco |

---

## 2. Steps in Designing a Database

1. **Requirements Analysis:**
   - Identify what data needs to be stored and retrieved.
2. **Conceptual Design:**
   - Create an Entity-Relationship (ER) diagram.

- Define entities, attributes, and relationships.

3. **Logical Design:**
    - Convert the ER diagram into tables.
    - Specify primary keys (PK) and foreign keys (FK).
4. **Normalization:**
    - Apply normalization rules to remove redundancy.
5. **Physical Design:**
    - Define storage, indexing, and optimization strategies.

*Example:*

**ER Diagram:** Entities: Employee, Department
Relationships: An Employee belongs to a Department.

---

## 3. Normal Forms

Normalization organizes data to reduce redundancy and dependency. Below are common normal forms:

*First Normal Form (1NF):*

**Rule:** Eliminate repeating groups; ensure each column has atomic values.

**Example: Unnormalized Table:**

```
| StudentID | Name      | Subjects        |
|-----------|-----------|-----------------|
| 1         | Alice     | Math, Science   |
| 2         | Bob       | Math, English   |
```

**1NF Table:**

```
| StudentID | Name   | Subject    |
|-----------|--------|------------|
| 1         | Alice  | Math       |
| 1         | Alice  | Science    |
| 2         | Bob    | Math       |
| 2         | Bob    | English    |
```

---

### *Second Normal Form (2NF):*

**Rule:** Ensure no partial dependency; move attributes dependent only on part of the primary key to a separate table.

**Example: 1NF Table:**

| OrderID | ProductID | ProductName | Quantity |
|---|---|---|---|
| 1 | 101 | Widget A | 5 |
| 2 | 102 | Widget B | 3 |

**2NF Tables:**

1. **Orders Table:**

| OrderID | ProductID | Quantity |
|---|---|---|
| 1 | 101 | 5 |
| 2 | 102 | 3 |

2. **Products Table:**

| ProductID | ProductName |
|---|---|
| 101 | Widget A |
| 102 | Widget B |

---

### *Third Normal Form (3NF):*

**Rule:** Eliminate transitive dependencies.

**Example: 2NF Table:**

| EmpID | Name | DeptID | DeptName |
|---|---|---|---|
| 1 | Alice | 10 | HR |
| 2 | Bob | 20 | IT |

**3NF Tables:**

1. **Employee Table:**

| EmpID | Name | DeptID |
|---|---|---|
| 1 | Alice | 10 |
| 2 | Bob | 20 |

2. **Department Table:**

```
| DeptID | DeptName   |
|--------|-----------|
| 10     | HR        |
| 20     | IT        |
```

---

*Boyce-Codd Normal Form (BCNF):*

**Rule:** Ensure no non-prime attribute determines a primary key.

**Example: 3NF Table Violating BCNF:**

```
| StudentID | CourseID | Instructor |
|-----------|----------|------------|
| 1         | 101      | Prof. A    |
| 2         | 102      | Prof. B    |
```

**BCNF Tables:**

1. **StudentCourse Table:**

```
| StudentID | CourseID |
|-----------|----------|
| 1         | 101      |
| 2         | 102      |
```

2. **CourseInstructor Table:**

```
| CourseID | Instructor |
|----------|------------|
| 101      | Prof. A    |
| 102      | Prof. B    |
```

---

## 4. Denormalization Techniques

**Denormalization** involves combining tables to improve query performance at the cost of redundancy.

*Example:*

**Normalized:** Separate tables for orders and customers.

**Denormalized:** Combine them into one table for faster lookups:

| OrderID | CustomerName | Product | Quantity |
|---|---|---|---|
| 1 | Alice | Widget A | 2 |
| 2 | Bob | Widget B | 1 |

---

## Common Database Design Pitfalls and How to Avoid Them

Designing an efficient database involves avoiding common pitfalls that can compromise data integrity, query performance, and scalability. Below are detailed explanations of these pitfalls, along with solutions and examples.

---

## 1. Redundancy

*Pitfall:*

Storing duplicate data across tables or within the same table, leading to inconsistencies, increased storage usage, and maintenance challenges.

*Example of Redundancy:*

**Redundant Table:**

| EmpID | Name | DeptName | DeptLocation |
|---|---|---|---|
| 1 | Alice | HR | New York |
| 2 | Bob | IT | San Francisco |
| 3 | Charlie | HR | New York |

- **Problem:** The department name and location are repeated for every employee in the same department.

*Solution:*

Apply **normalization** to separate related data into distinct tables, ensuring data consistency and reducing redundancy.

**Normalized Tables:**

1. **Employee Table:**

| EmpID | Name | DeptID |
|---|---|---|
| 1 | Alice | 1 |
| 2 | Bob | 2 |
| 3 | Charlie | 1 |

2. **Department Table:**

| DeptID | DeptName | DeptLocation |
|---|---|---|
| 1 | HR | New York |
| 2 | IT | San Francisco |

---

## 2. Poor Naming Conventions

*Pitfall:*

Using ambiguous or inconsistent names for tables and columns, making it difficult for developers and analysts to understand the data model.

*Example of Poor Naming:*

| ID | Nm | Dept |
|---|---|---|
| 1 | Alice | HR |
| 2 | Bob | IT |

- **Problem:** The column names `ID`, `Nm`, and `Dept` are unclear, and the purpose of the table is not obvious.

*Solution:*

Use **descriptive and consistent names** that clearly indicate the table's purpose and the data stored in each column.

**Improved Table:**

| EmployeeID | EmployeeName | DepartmentName |
|---|---|---|
| 1 | Alice | HR |
| 2 | Bob | IT |

---

## 3. Lack of Constraints

*Pitfall:*

Failing to define **Primary Keys**, **Foreign Keys**, or other constraints can lead to data inconsistency, duplication, or invalid relationships between tables.

*Example of Missing Constraints:*

| OrderID | CustomerName | Product |
|---|---|---|
| 1 | Alice | Widget A |
| 1 | Bob | Widget B |

- **Problem:** Duplicate `OrderID` values indicate a lack of a primary key.

*Solution:*

Define constraints to enforce data integrity.

- **Primary Key:** Ensures each row is unique.
- **Foreign Key:** Maintains referential integrity between related tables.
- **Check Constraints:** Validates specific column values.

**Improved Tables:**

1. **Orders Table:**

| OrderID | CustomerID | ProductID |
|---|---|---|
| 1 | 101 | 1001 |

   - Primary Key: `OrderID`.

2. **Customers Table:**

| CustomerID | CustomerName |
|---|---|
| 101 | Alice |

   - Foreign Key: `CustomerID` in the `Orders` table references `CustomerID`.

## 4. Over-Normalization

*Pitfall:*

Dividing data into too many small tables can make queries overly complex and degrade performance, especially for read-heavy applications.

*Example of Over-Normalization:*

**Highly Normalized Design:**

1. **Employee Table:**

| EmpID | NameID |
|-------|--------|
| 1 | 101 |

2. **Name Table:**

| NameID | FirstName | LastName |
|--------|-----------|----------|
| 101 | Alice | Smith |

- **Problem:** Simple queries like fetching employee names require multiple joins.

*Solution:*

Use **denormalization** to merge frequently accessed data into a single table for better performance.

**Denormalized Table:**

| EmpID | FirstName | LastName |
|-------|-----------|----------|
| 1 | Alice | Smith |

## 5. Ignoring Future Growth

*Pitfall:*

Not planning for scalability can lead to performance bottlenecks as the database grows in size.

*Example of Scalability Issues:*

A table designed without indexing:

```
| EmpID | Name    | DeptName |
|-------|---------|----------|
| 1     | Alice   | HR       |
| 2     | Bob     | IT       |
| ...   | ...     | ...      |
```

- **Problem:** Searching for specific employees in a table with millions of rows becomes slow.

*Solution:*

- **Anticipate Growth:** Estimate future data size and structure tables accordingly.
- **Plan Indexing:** Create indexes on frequently queried columns for faster lookups.
- **Partitioning:** Split large tables into smaller partitions based on criteria like date or region.

### Example with Indexing:

```
CREATE INDEX idx_employee_name ON Employees (Name);
```

- Improves query performance for searches like:

```
SELECT * FROM Employees WHERE Name = 'Alice';
```

---

## Summary of Solutions:

| Pitfall | Solution |
|---|---|
| Redundancy | Normalize tables to eliminate duplicate data. |
| Poor Naming Conventions | Use descriptive and consistent naming. |
| Lack of Constraints | Define primary and foreign keys, use constraints. |
| Over-Normalization | Use denormalization for read-heavy applications. |
| Ignoring Future Growth | Plan indexing and anticipate scalability. |

## 1. Principles of Database Design: Ensuring Data Integrity

**Scenario:** A database for a university stores student data.

### Example: Table Design:

| StudentID | Name | Email | Course |
|---|---|---|---|
| 1 | Alice | alice@example.com | CS101 |
| 2 | Bob | bob@example.com | CS101 |
| 3 | Charlie | charlie@example.com | CS102 |

**Principle Applied:** Define **Primary Key** and **Unique Constraints** to ensure data integrity.

```
ALTER TABLE Students ADD CONSTRAINT PK_StudentID PRIMARY KEY (StudentID);
ALTER TABLE Students ADD CONSTRAINT UC_Email UNIQUE (Email);
```

### Output:

- Ensures no duplicate student IDs or emails are entered.

---

## 2. Steps in Designing a Database: Identifying Entities and Relationships

**Scenario:** A library system tracks books and borrowers.

### Steps Applied:

1. Identify entities: `Books`, `Borrowers`, and `Loans`.
2. Define relationships: Borrowers can borrow multiple books.
3. Design tables.

### Example Design: Books Table:

| BookID | Title | Author |
|---|---|---|
| 1 | Database Design | John Smith |
| 2 | Algorithms | Alice Johnson |

### Borrowers Table:

| BorrowerID | Name | Email |
|---|---|---|
| 1 | Alice | alice@example.com |
| 2 | Bob | bob@example.com |

**Loans Table (Relationship):**

| LoanID | BorrowerID | BookID | DateBorrowed |
|---|---|---|---|
| 1 | 1 | 2 | 2024-12-01 |
| 2 | 2 | 1 | 2024-12-02 |

---

## 3. First Normal Form (1NF)

**Scenario:** Student table with multiple phone numbers stored in a single column.

**Non-1NF Table:**

| StudentID | Name | PhoneNumbers |
|---|---|---|
| 1 | Alice | 1234567890,9876543210 |

**Normalized Table (1NF):**

| StudentID | Name | PhoneNumber |
|---|---|---|
| 1 | Alice | 1234567890 |
| 1 | Alice | 9876543210 |

**Explanation:** Split multivalued columns into separate rows to achieve 1NF.

---

## 4. Second Normal Form (2NF)

**Scenario:** A student-course table with partial dependency.

**Non-2NF Table:**

| StudentID | CourseID | CourseName |
|---|---|---|
| 1 | CS101 | Databases |
| 2 | CS102 | Algorithms |

**Normalized Tables:**

1. **Student-Course Table:**

| StudentID | CourseID |
|---|---|
| 1 | CS101 |
| 2 | CS102 |

2. **Course Table:**

| CourseID | CourseName |
|---|---|
| CS101 | Databases |
| CS102 | Algorithms |

**Explanation:** Remove partial dependency by creating separate tables.

---

## 5. Third Normal Form (3NF)

**Scenario:** Employee table with transitive dependency.

**Non-3NF Table:**

| EmpID | Name | DeptID | DeptName |
|---|---|---|---|
| 1 | Alice | 101 | HR |
| 2 | Bob | 102 | IT |

**Normalized Tables:**

1. **Employee Table:**

| EmpID | Name | DeptID |
|---|---|---|
| 1 | Alice | 101 |
| 2 | Bob | 102 |

2. **Department Table:**

| DeptID | DeptName |
|---|---|
| 101 | HR |
| 102 | IT |

**Explanation:** Remove transitive dependency by separating department details.

---

## 6. Boyce-Codd Normal Form (BCNF)

**Scenario:** Functional dependency violation in a table of student preferences.

**Non-BCNF Table:**

| StudentID | CourseID | Preference |
|-----------|----------|------------|
| 1 | CS101 | High |
| 2 | CS102 | Medium |

- Problem: `Preference` depends on both `StudentID` and `CourseID`.

**Solution:** Break into smaller tables to achieve BCNF.

---

## 7. Denormalization Techniques

**Scenario:** Combining tables for performance in a read-heavy application.

**Normalized Design:**

1. **Orders Table:**

   | OrderID | CustomerID |

2. **Customer Table:**

   | CustomerID | Name |

**Denormalized Table:**

| OrderID | CustomerID | Name |
|---------|------------|-------|
| 1 | 101 | Alice |

---

## 8. Common Design Pitfall: Redundancy

**Scenario:** Storing duplicate department information.

**Redundant Table:**

| EmpID | Name | DeptName |
|-------|--------|----------|
| 1 | Alice | HR |
| 2 | Bob | HR |

**Solution:** Normalize into two tables:

- Employees
- Departments

---

## 9. Common Design Pitfall: Poor Naming Conventions

**Scenario:** Ambiguous table names like `Tbl1`.

**Solution:** Rename to meaningful names like `EmployeeDetails`.

---

## 10. Common Design Pitfall: Lack of Constraints

**Scenario:** No primary key in an orders table.

**Non-Constrained Table:**

```
| OrderID | Product    |
|---------|------------|
| 1       | Widget A   |
| 1       | Widget B   |
```

**Solution:** Define `OrderID` as a primary key to prevent duplicates.

```
ALTER TABLE Orders ADD CONSTRAINT PK_Order PRIMARY KEY (OrderID);
```

# CHAPTER-9

## INDEXING AND PERFORMANCE OPTIMIZATION

## 1. Introduction to Indexes

An **index** is a database structure that improves the speed of data retrieval operations on a table by creating a sorted copy of specified columns.

**Example without Index:** Consider a table `Employees` with thousands of rows:

```
| EmpID | Name         | Department |
|-------|------------|------------|
| 1     | Alice        | HR         |
| 2     | Bob          | IT         |
| ...   | ...          | ...        |
```

A query like:

```
SELECT * FROM Employees WHERE Name = 'Alice';
```

performs a **full table scan**, checking each row.

**Example with Index:** Adding an index on the `Name` column:

```
CREATE INDEX idx_name ON Employees(Name);
```

The query now uses the index to find rows, significantly reducing search time.

**Key Advantages:**

- Faster SELECT queries.
- Improved data retrieval efficiency.

---

## 2. Types of Indexes

### 2.1 Clustered Index

- Determines the physical order of data in a table.
- Each table can have only one clustered index.

**Example:** Creating a clustered index on `EmpID`:

```
CREATE CLUSTERED INDEX idx_empid ON Employees(EmpID);
```

Data is physically ordered by `EmpID`.

---

### 2.2 Non-Clustered Index

- Creates a separate structure for the index; data is not physically ordered.
- A table can have multiple non-clustered indexes.

**Example:** Creating a non-clustered index on `Name`:

```
CREATE NONCLUSTERED INDEX idx_name ON Employees(Name);
```

---

### 2.3 Composite Index

- Index on multiple columns.

**Example:** Creating a composite index on `Name` and `Department`:

```
CREATE INDEX idx_name_dept ON Employees(Name, Department);
```

Used for queries like:

```
SELECT * FROM Employees WHERE Name = 'Alice' AND Department = 'HR';
```

---

## 3. Understanding Query Execution Plans

A **query execution plan** shows how a database executes a query. It helps identify inefficiencies.

**Example:**

```
SELECT * FROM Employees WHERE Name = 'Alice';
```

Using tools like `EXPLAIN` in MySQL or `Query Analyzer` in SQL Server, you can view:

- Indexes used.
- Full table scans.
- Estimated vs. actual rows processed.

**Visual Output:**

- A graphical query plan highlights which steps take the most time.

---

# 4. Tips for Query Optimization

*4.1 Use Indexes Wisely*

- Index columns used in `WHERE`, `JOIN`, and `ORDER BY`.

**Example:**

```
SELECT * FROM Orders WHERE OrderDate = '2024-12-01';
```

Create an index on `OrderDate`:

```
CREATE INDEX idx_orderdate ON Orders(OrderDate);
```

---

***4.2 Avoid SELECT ****

Fetching unnecessary columns increases overhead.

**Example (Inefficient):**

```
SELECT * FROM Employees;
```

**Optimized Query:**

```
SELECT EmpID, Name FROM Employees;
```

---

*4.3 Use LIMIT for Pagination*

For large datasets, fetch smaller chunks.

**Example:**

```
SELECT * FROM Employees LIMIT 10 OFFSET 20;
```

---

*4.4 Optimize Joins*

- Ensure both joined columns are indexed.

**Example:**

```
SELECT e.Name, d.DeptName
FROM Employees e
JOIN Departments d ON e.DeptID = d.DeptID;
```

Index `DeptID` in both tables:

```
CREATE INDEX idx_emp_deptid ON Employees(DeptID);
CREATE INDEX idx_dept_deptid ON Departments(DeptID);
```

---

## 5. Avoiding Common Performance Issues

Database performance is essential for responsive applications. Poor practices, such as missing indexes, inefficient queries, and large transactions, can degrade performance. Below are some common performance issues, their causes, and solutions, with explanations and examples.

---

### 5.1 Missing Indexes

*Issue: Slow Queries Due to Full Table Scans*

When a query lacks an index, the database performs a **full table scan**, inspecting every row, which is inefficient for large datasets.

**Example:** Consider a table `Employees` with 1 million rows:

```
SELECT * FROM Employees WHERE Department = 'HR';
```

Without an index on the `Department` column, the database scans all rows.

**Solution: Identify slow queries and add indexes.**

1. Use tools like **EXPLAIN** (MySQL) or **Execution Plans** (SQL Server) to find queries that perform full table scans.
2. Create an index:

   ```
   CREATE INDEX idx_department ON Employees(Department);
   ```

   This reduces the search space, as the database can quickly locate rows in the `Department` index.

---

## 5.2 Over-Indexing

*Issue: Too Many Indexes Slow Down INSERT/UPDATE Operations*

Indexes improve query speed but slow down data modifications like `INSERT` and `UPDATE`, as all related indexes must also be updated.

**Example:** If `Employees` has indexes on `Name`, `Department`, `Salary`, and `HireDate`, inserting a new row involves updating all these indexes.

**Solution: Use only necessary indexes.**

1. Analyze query patterns and only index frequently searched columns.
2. Remove unused indexes:

```
DROP INDEX idx_unused ON Employees;
```

Focus on high-impact indexes for critical queries.

---

## 5.3 Ignoring Query Execution Plans

*Issue: Inefficient Queries with High Cost*

Query execution plans show the steps a database takes to execute a query. Ignoring them can result in inefficient queries with high execution costs.

**Example:**

```
SELECT * FROM Orders WHERE OrderDate BETWEEN '2024-01-01' AND '2024-12-31';
```

If there's no index on `OrderDate`, the query may perform a full table scan.

**Solution: Regularly review and optimize plans.**

1. Use tools like **EXPLAIN** or **SET STATISTICS TIME** to analyze queries.
2. Add indexes or rewrite queries to reduce cost:

```
CREATE INDEX idx_orderdate ON Orders(OrderDate);
```

**Output:** Query plans before and after optimization show reduced cost and improved efficiency.

---

## 5.4 Unoptimized Joins

*Issue: Joining Non-Indexed Columns*

Joins between tables without proper indexes are computationally expensive, especially for large datasets.

**Example:**

```
SELECT e.Name, d.DeptName
FROM Employees e
JOIN Departments d ON e.DeptID = d.DeptID;
```

If `DeptID` is not indexed in either table, the database performs a full scan on both tables.

**Solution: Ensure proper indexes.**

1. Index columns used in joins:

   ```
   CREATE INDEX idx_emp_deptid ON Employees(DeptID);
   CREATE INDEX idx_dept_deptid ON Departments(DeptID);
   ```

2. Query now uses indexes, reducing join time.

---

## 5.5 Large Transactions

*Issue: Transactions Locking Rows or Tables*

Large transactions can lock rows or entire tables, blocking other operations and causing performance bottlenecks.

**Example:**

```
BEGIN TRANSACTION;
UPDATE Employees SET Salary = Salary * 1.1 WHERE Department = 'IT';
DELETE FROM Employees WHERE Department = 'HR';
COMMIT;
```

If this transaction affects thousands of rows, it locks the table until completion.

**Solution: Break transactions into smaller parts.**

1. Use batches for large updates:

   ```
   UPDATE Employees
   SET Salary = Salary * 1.1
   ```

```
WHERE Department = 'IT'
LIMIT 1000;
```

2. Commit changes in smaller chunks to release locks:

```
BEGIN TRANSACTION;
-- First Batch
UPDATE Employees SET Salary = Salary * 1.1 WHERE Department = 'IT'
LIMIT 500;
COMMIT;

BEGIN TRANSACTION;
-- Second Batch
UPDATE Employees SET Salary = Salary * 1.1 WHERE Department = 'IT'
LIMIT 500;
COMMIT;
```

---

## 1. Introduction to Indexes: Improving Query Performance

**Scenario: Searching a specific record in a large table.**

**Query Without Index:**

```
SELECT * FROM Employees WHERE EmployeeID = 101;
```

- **Execution Time:** 500ms (full table scan).

**Solution: Create an index on EmployeeID.**

```
CREATE INDEX idx_employee_id ON Employees(EmployeeID);
```

**Query With Index:**

```
SELECT * FROM Employees WHERE EmployeeID = 101;
```

- **Execution Time:** 10ms (index scan).

---

## 2. Clustered Index: Optimizing Range Queries

**Scenario: Fetching records based on date range.**

**Table Structure:**

- `Orders(OrderID, OrderDate, CustomerID)`

**Create Clustered Index:**

```
CREATE CLUSTERED INDEX idx_orderdate ON Orders(OrderDate);
```

**Query:**

```
SELECT * FROM Orders WHERE OrderDate BETWEEN '2024-01-01' AND '2024-12-31';
```

- **Execution Time:** Reduced significantly due to ordered storage of data.

## 3. Non-Clustered Index: Searching Specific Columns

**Scenario: Searching by CustomerID in `Orders`.**

**Create Non-Clustered Index:**

```
CREATE NONCLUSTERED INDEX idx_customer_id ON Orders(CustomerID);
```

**Query:**

```
SELECT * FROM Orders WHERE CustomerID = 12345;
```

- **Result:** Improved query speed as only the relevant rows are accessed.

---

## 4. Composite Index: Optimizing Multi-Column Searches

**Scenario: Searching by multiple columns.**

**Create Composite Index:**

```
CREATE INDEX idx_customer_date ON Orders(CustomerID, OrderDate);
```

**Query:**

```
SELECT * FROM Orders WHERE CustomerID = 12345 AND OrderDate > '2024-01-01';
```

- **Execution Plan:** Combines CustomerID and OrderDate for faster lookups.

---

## 5. Query Execution Plan Analysis

**Scenario: Analyzing query performance using `EXPLAIN`.**

**Query:**

```
EXPLAIN SELECT * FROM Employees WHERE Department = 'HR';
```

**Output:**

- Full table scan shown due to missing index.

**Solution:**

```
CREATE INDEX idx_department ON Employees(Department);
```

**Improved Execution Plan:**

- Uses the `idx_department` index for faster lookups.

---

## 6. Optimizing LIKE Queries with Indexes

**Scenario: Searching names starting with 'A'.**

**Query Without Index:**

```
SELECT * FROM Employees WHERE Name LIKE 'A%';
```

**Solution:**

```
CREATE INDEX idx_name ON Employees(Name);
```

**Query With Index:**

```
SELECT * FROM Employees WHERE Name LIKE 'A%';
```

- **Execution Time:** Significantly reduced.

---

## 7. Avoiding Over-Indexing

**Scenario: Table has redundant indexes.**

**Initial Indexes:**

- `idx_name`
- `idx_name_dept`

**Query:**

```
SELECT Name, Department FROM Employees WHERE Name = 'John';
```

**Solution:** Keep only `idx_name_dept` as it covers both columns:

```
DROP INDEX idx_name;
```

---

## 8. Covering Index

**Scenario: Selecting indexed columns.**

**Create Covering Index:**

```
CREATE INDEX idx_salary ON Employees(Salary) INCLUDE (Name, Department);
```

**Query:**

```
SELECT Name, Department FROM Employees WHERE Salary > 50000;
```

- **Performance:** Faster as all data is fetched directly from the index.

---

## 9. Optimizing JOIN Queries

**Scenario: Joining two large tables.**

**Tables:**

- `Employees(EmployeeID, DepartmentID)`
- `Departments(DepartmentID, DepartmentName)`

**Query:**

```
SELECT e.Name, d.DepartmentName
FROM Employees e
JOIN Departments d ON e.DepartmentID = d.DepartmentID;
```

**Solution: Index `DepartmentID` in both tables:**

```
CREATE INDEX idx_emp_deptid ON Employees(DepartmentID);
CREATE INDEX idx_dept_deptid ON Departments(DepartmentID);
```

---

## 10. Partial Indexes

**Scenario: Indexing only specific data.**

**Create Partial Index:**

```
CREATE INDEX idx_active_emp ON Employees(Status) WHERE Status = 'Active';
```

**Query:**

```
SELECT * FROM Employees WHERE Status = 'Active';
```

- **Performance:** Optimized by indexing only relevant rows.

---

## 11. Indexing Foreign Keys

**Scenario: Optimizing foreign key lookups.**

**Create Index:**

```
CREATE INDEX idx_fk_customer ON Orders(CustomerID);
```

**Query:**

```
SELECT * FROM Orders WHERE CustomerID = 12345;
```

- **Result:** Faster queries due to indexed foreign key.

---

## 12. Dropping Unused Indexes

**Scenario: Removing unnecessary indexes.**

**Identify Unused Indexes:**

```
SELECT * FROM sys.dm_db_index_usage_stats;
```

**Solution: Drop unused indexes:**

```
DROP INDEX idx_unused ON Employees;
```

---

## 13. Breaking Down Large Transactions

### Scenario: Large updates locking rows.

### Initial Query:

```
UPDATE Employees SET Salary = Salary * 1.1 WHERE Department = 'HR';
```

**Optimized Solution:** Break into smaller transactions:

```
UPDATE Employees SET Salary = Salary * 1.1 WHERE Department = 'HR' LIMIT
1000;
```

---

## 14. Indexing for Aggregate Queries

### Scenario: Counting rows in a specific department.

### Query Without Index:

```
SELECT COUNT(*) FROM Employees WHERE Department = 'HR';
```

### Solution:

```
CREATE INDEX idx_department ON Employees(Department);
```

### Query With Index:

```
SELECT COUNT(*) FROM Employees WHERE Department = 'HR';
```

- **Performance:** Faster aggregate calculation.

---

## 15. Avoiding Fragmentation

### Scenario: Indexes become fragmented over time.

### Detect Fragmentation:

```
SELECT * FROM sys.dm_db_index_physical_stats(NULL, NULL, NULL, NULL,
'DETAILED');
```

### Solution: Rebuild indexes:

```
ALTER INDEX idx_department ON Employees REBUILD;
```

## Summary Table

| Topic | Key Point |
|---|---|
| Introduction to Indexes | Speed up data retrieval, e.g., `CREATE INDEX idx_name ON Employees(Name);` |
| Clustered Index | Data physically ordered by indexed column, one per table. |
| Non-Clustered Index | Separate structure for index, allows multiple indexes. |
| Composite Index | Index on multiple columns for multi-condition queries. |
| Query Execution Plans | Analyze database's query execution strategy. |
| Tips for Query Optimization | Index important columns, avoid `SELECT *`, optimize joins. |
| Avoiding Common Performance Issues | Add necessary indexes, avoid over-indexing, review execution plans. |

# CHAPTER-10

## TRANSACTIONS AND CONCURRENCY CONTROL

### 1. What is a Transaction?

A **transaction** in a database is a group of operations that are treated as a single logical unit. These operations must either be executed completely or not at all to ensure data integrity and consistency.

---

### Key Concepts of Transactions

1. **Start Transaction:**
    - Initiates the sequence of operations that form the transaction.
    - The database starts tracking changes made during the transaction.
2. **Commit:**
    - Finalizes the transaction.
    - All changes made during the transaction are permanently saved to the database.
    - Ensures data is consistent and available for other transactions.
3. **Rollback:**
    - Cancels the transaction if an error occurs.
    - Reverts the database to its state before the transaction began, ensuring no partial or erroneous data changes.

---

### Example: Transferring Money Between Accounts

**Scenario:**
Transfer $100 from Account A (AccountID = 1) to Account B (AccountID = 2).

1. **Operation Details:**
    - Deduct $100 from Account A.
    - Add $100 to Account B.
    - Commit changes only if both operations succeed.

**SQL Implementation:**

```
START TRANSACTION;

-- Deduct $100 from Account A
UPDATE Accounts SET Balance = Balance - 100 WHERE AccountID = 1;
```

```
-- Add $100 to Account B
UPDATE Accounts SET Balance = Balance + 100 WHERE AccountID = 2;

-- Commit the transaction to make changes permanent
COMMIT;
```

**Expected Results:**

- Before the transaction:
  - Account A Balance: $500
  - Account B Balance: $300
- After the transaction:
  - Account A Balance: $400
  - Account B Balance: $400

---

## What Happens if an Error Occurs?

If any part of the transaction fails (e.g., insufficient funds in Account A or a database connection issue), the entire transaction is rolled back to maintain data integrity.

**SQL with Rollback:**

```
START TRANSACTION;

-- Deduct $100 from Account A
UPDATE Accounts SET Balance = Balance - 100 WHERE AccountID = 1;

-- Simulate an error in the second operation
UPDATE Accounts SET Balance = Balance + 100 WHERE AccountID = 2;

-- If an error occurs, rollback the transaction
ROLLBACK;
```

**Outcome in Case of Rollback:**

- No changes are applied to either account.
- Account A Balance: $500
- Account B Balance: $300

---

## Properties of Transactions

Transactions adhere to **ACID** properties:

1. **Atomicity:** Ensures all operations in the transaction are completed, or none are.

2. **Consistency:** Guarantees the database remains in a valid state before and after the transaction.
3. **Isolation:** Prevents interference between concurrent transactions.
4. **Durability:** Ensures committed changes are permanent, even in the event of a system failure.

---

## 2. ACID Properties

## ACID Properties of Database Transactions

The **ACID** properties are a set of principles that guarantee reliable processing of database transactions, ensuring that the database remains in a consistent and valid state, even in the face of system crashes, hardware failures, or other unexpected events.

ACID stands for:

1. **Atomicity**
2. **Consistency**
3. **Isolation**
4. **Durability**

These properties work together to ensure that database transactions are processed in a reliable and predictable manner.

---

## 1. Atomicity

- **Definition:** Atomicity ensures that a transaction is treated as a single, indivisible unit. Either all operations in a transaction are executed successfully, or none are. If any part of the transaction fails, the entire transaction is rolled back to its original state.
- **How it Works:**
  - If one operation in a transaction fails, the database undoes (rolls back) all operations performed by the transaction to maintain consistency.
  - This prevents the database from being left in an incomplete or corrupted state.

*Example:*

**Scenario:** Transferring $100 from Account A to Account B.

**Before Transaction:**

- Account A: $500
- Account B: $300

**Operations in Transaction:**

- Deduct $100 from Account A.
- Add $100 to Account B.

**If an error occurs after deducting from Account A but before adding to Account B:**

- Account A would be $400, but Account B would still be $300.
- **Rollback:** The database would roll back both operations, and the balances would remain unchanged:
    - Account A: $500
    - Account B: $300

**Commit:** If both operations succeed, the transaction commits, and the balances would update as expected:

- Account A: $400
- Account B: $400

---

## 2. Consistency

- **Definition:** Consistency ensures that the database moves from one valid state to another valid state before and after the transaction. The transaction must leave the database in a valid state according to all defined rules, constraints, and triggers.
- **How it Works:**
    - The database must adhere to all defined integrity constraints (e.g., primary keys, foreign keys, check constraints).
    - Any operation that violates these constraints is prevented, and the transaction is rolled back.

*Example:*

Consider a table `Accounts` with a constraint that the `Balance` must never be negative.

- **Before Transaction:**
    - Account A: $500
    - Account B: $300
- **Transaction:** Transfer $100 from Account A to Account B.
    - Deduct $100 from Account A (New Balance: $400).
    - Add $100 to Account B (New Balance: $400).
- **If the transaction is consistent:**
    - The total balance before and after remains the same.
    - Account A and Account B are both valid.

However, if the transaction tries to deduct more money than is available in Account A:

- **Rollback:** The transaction fails to maintain consistency (Account A cannot have a negative balance), so it is rolled back.

---

## 3. Isolation

- **Definition:** Isolation ensures that concurrently executing transactions do not interfere with each other. Each transaction is isolated from others until it is completed, ensuring that the final result of the database is as if the transactions were executed one after another, rather than concurrently.
- **How it Works:**
    - The isolation level of a transaction controls how visible its operations are to other transactions. The higher the isolation level, the less interference there is between transactions, but this can reduce system performance due to locking.
- **Isolation Levels:**

0. **Read Uncommitted**: Allows reading uncommitted changes from other transactions (can cause dirty reads).
1. **Read Committed**: Only committed data is visible, preventing dirty reads but allowing non-repeatable reads.
2. **Repeatable Read**: Ensures that if a transaction reads a value, it will see the same value if it reads it again within the transaction (prevents non-repeatable reads).
3. **Serializable**: The highest isolation level. Transactions are executed serially, one after another, preventing all types of anomalies.

*Example:*

Two transactions are running simultaneously:

- **Transaction 1:** Transfers $100 from Account A to Account B.
- **Transaction 2:** Reads the balance of Account A while Transaction 1 is modifying it.

With **Read Committed Isolation**:

- Transaction 2 will only see Account A's balance before Transaction 1 commits (avoiding inconsistent or "dirty" reads).

---

## 4. Durability

- **Definition:** Durability ensures that once a transaction has been committed, its changes are permanent, even if there is a system crash or power failure. The data is written to non-volatile storage (such as a disk), making it safe from loss.
- **How it Works:**

- Once a transaction is committed, its effects are permanent, regardless of any system failure.
- The changes are saved to the disk, and recovery mechanisms are in place to restore the database to a consistent state in case of unexpected interruptions.

*Example:*

- **Before Transaction:**
  - Account A: $500
  - Account B: $300
- **Transaction:** Transfer $100 from Account A to Account B.
  - Deduct $100 from Account A (New Balance: $400).
  - Add $100 to Account B (New Balance: $400).
- **System Crash Occurs Before Commit:**
  - If the system crashes before the commit, the transaction will not be finalized, and the changes will be lost.
  - **After Recovery:** The balances will remain as they were before the transaction:
    - Account A: $500
    - Account B: $300
- **After Commit:** If the transaction commits before a crash, the changes to the database are guaranteed:
  - Account A: $400
  - Account B: $400
  - Even in the event of a failure, the changes will be preserved after recovery.

---

## 3. Isolation Levels

Isolation levels define the degree to which the operations of one transaction are isolated from those of another. Higher isolation levels provide more consistency but may reduce performance.

| Isolation Level | Description | Potential Issues |
|---|---|---|
| **Read Uncommitted** | Allows reading uncommitted changes. | Dirty reads. |
| **Read Committed** | Only committed changes are visible. | Non-repeatable reads. |
| **Repeatable Read** | Ensures consistent reads during a transaction. | Phantom reads. |
| **Serializable** | Full isolation; highest consistency. | Slower performance. |

*Example:*

**Scenario:** Two transactions access the same data.

sql

```
START TRANSACTION;
SELECT * FROM Accounts WHERE AccountID = 1 FOR UPDATE;
-- No other transaction can modify AccountID 1 until this completes.
COMMIT;
```

---

## 4. Handling Deadlocks

A **deadlock** occurs when two or more transactions are stuck in a cycle, each waiting for the other to release a resource, resulting in a situation where none of the transactions can proceed. This can happen when transactions hold locks on some resources and request locks on others, but those requested resources are already locked by other transactions. As a result, all the transactions involved are blocked indefinitely.

*Example of Deadlock:*

Consider two transactions operating on two rows of a table:

- **Transaction 1** locks **Row A** and tries to lock **Row B**.
- **Transaction 2** locks **Row B** and tries to lock **Row A**.

In this scenario:

- **Transaction 1** is holding a lock on **Row A** and waiting for **Row B** to be released by **Transaction 2**.
- **Transaction 2** is holding a lock on **Row B** and waiting for **Row A** to be released by **Transaction 1**.

This forms a cycle where both transactions are waiting for each other to release locks, and neither can proceed. This situation is a **deadlock**.

### Solutions to Handle Deadlocks

Several strategies are employed to detect, avoid, or recover from deadlocks in database systems:

*1. Timeouts:*

- **Description:** A **timeout** is one way to handle deadlocks. If a transaction is waiting for a lock for too long, it is aborted, and the system automatically retries or rolls back the transaction to prevent a deadlock scenario from continuing indefinitely.
- **How it Works:** If a transaction waits for a lock for a specified period, and no lock is granted during that time, the transaction is considered as "timed out." It will be rolled back, allowing the other transactions to proceed.
- **Example:**
    - Transaction 1 attempts to acquire a lock on **Row A** and proceeds to acquire a lock on **Row B**.
    - Transaction 2 attempts to acquire a lock on **Row B** and proceeds to acquire a lock on **Row A**.

- If neither of the transactions gets their second lock within a predefined timeout period (e.g., 30 seconds), both transactions will be rolled back, and the resources are freed.

- **SQL Example:**

```
SET LOCK_TIMEOUT 30; -- Wait for a lock for 30 seconds
BEGIN TRANSACTION;
-- Lock operations go here
COMMIT;
```

- **Result:** If the lock cannot be acquired within 30 seconds, the transaction is rolled back automatically.

*2. Deadlock Detection and Resolution:*

- **Description:** Deadlock detection is a method where the system periodically checks for deadlocks. If a deadlock is detected, the system resolves the situation by **rolling back one of the transactions**, allowing the other transaction(s) to proceed.
- **How it Works:** The database system maintains a **wait-for graph**, which tracks transactions and the resources they are waiting for. If a cycle is detected in this graph, it indicates a deadlock. Once a deadlock is detected, the system chooses one of the transactions involved in the cycle and rolls it back to break the deadlock.
- **Steps in Deadlock Detection:**
  1. The system detects the cycle in the **wait-for graph**.
  2. The system chooses one transaction to roll back based on a predefined rule, such as the one with the least amount of work done or the one that has been waiting the longest.
  3. The rolled-back transaction releases its locks, allowing the other transactions to proceed.
- **Example:**
  - Transaction 1 locks **Row A** and waits for **Row B**.
  - Transaction 2 locks **Row B** and waits for **Row A**.
  - The system detects a cycle in the wait-for graph.
  - The system rolls back **Transaction 2**, releasing its lock on **Row B**, so **Transaction 1** can proceed with its operations.
- **SQL Example:**
  - This is typically handled by the DBMS automatically. However, it can be explicitly queried using:

```
SHOW ENGINE INNODB STATUS; -- In MySQL to check deadlock status
```

- **Result:** Deadlock is detected, and **Transaction 2** is rolled back, releasing the locks and allowing **Transaction 1** to continue.

*3. Resource Ordering:*

- **Description:** Resource ordering is a strategy where transactions acquire locks in a predefined order. This ensures that circular waiting cannot occur, because no transaction can hold one resource while waiting for a resource that is locked by another transaction.

- **How it Works:**
  - All resources (rows, tables, etc.) are assigned a unique order or rank.
  - Transactions acquire locks in this specific order, ensuring that a transaction cannot hold a lock on a lower-ranked resource while waiting for a higher-ranked resource.
  - This eliminates the possibility of circular dependencies between transactions, preventing deadlocks from occurring.
- **Example:**
  - Suppose resources (rows or tables) are ordered as **Row A** > **Row B** > **Row C**.
  - **Transaction 1** locks **Row A** and then tries to lock **Row B**.
  - **Transaction 2** locks **Row B** and then tries to lock **Row A**.
  - With resource ordering, **Transaction 2** would not be allowed to lock **Row A** while holding **Row B** since it violates the defined order.
- **SQL Example:**
  - Transaction 1:

```
BEGIN TRANSACTION;
LOCK TABLE Accounts IN EXCLUSIVE MODE; -- Lock in predefined
order
-- Perform operations
COMMIT;
```

- **Result:** By ensuring that all transactions acquire locks in a consistent and predetermined order, deadlocks are avoided.

---

## Best Practices to Handle Deadlocks:

1. **Short Transactions:**
   - Keep transactions as short as possible to reduce the window for deadlock occurrence. Short transactions acquire locks for less time and decrease the likelihood of conflict.
2. **Consistent Locking Order:**
   - Always acquire locks in the same order within all transactions to prevent circular dependencies.
3. **Minimize Lock Contention:**
   - Design the application so that transactions rarely need to access the same resources simultaneously.
4. **Retry Logic:**
   - Implement a retry mechanism where the application can attempt to complete the transaction again if it detects a deadlock.

---

## 5. Optimistic vs. Pessimistic Locking

## Optimistic vs. Pessimistic Locking in Database Systems

In database management systems (DBMS), **locking** is a mechanism used to prevent conflicting access to data by multiple transactions. The two primary approaches to locking are **pessimistic locking** and **optimistic locking**. Both have their own advantages and are used based on the nature of the transactions and the system's needs.

---

## 1. Pessimistic Locking

Pessimistic locking assumes that conflicts will occur, so it locks resources as soon as a transaction accesses the data. This approach prevents other transactions from modifying the same data, thereby ensuring consistency. However, it can significantly reduce the **concurrency** of the system because once a transaction holds a lock, other transactions must wait for the lock to be released before they can proceed.

*Key Characteristics:*

- **Locks are applied as soon as a transaction accesses the data.**
- **Prevents other transactions** from accessing or modifying the locked data.
- Ensures data integrity but can **reduce concurrency** as transactions are blocked until the lock is released.
- **Used in high-conflict environments** where consistency is a higher priority than concurrency.

*Example of Pessimistic Locking:*

Consider a banking system where two transactions are attempting to modify the balance of the same account at the same time:

1. **Transaction 1** wants to withdraw money from Account 1.
2. **Transaction 2** wants to withdraw money from Account 1 as well.

With **pessimistic locking**, the system locks the record immediately when it is accessed. For example, when Transaction 1 retrieves the account balance to update it, the row will be locked, preventing Transaction 2 from accessing the same account until Transaction 1 is completed.

```
START TRANSACTION;
SELECT * FROM Accounts WHERE AccountID = 1 FOR UPDATE;
-- The row for Account 1 is locked for Transaction 1.
UPDATE Accounts SET Balance = Balance - 100 WHERE AccountID = 1;
COMMIT;
```

- In this case, the `FOR UPDATE` clause locks the selected row. While **Transaction 1** is updating Account 1, **Transaction 2** will be blocked from making any changes to that account until **Transaction 1** completes.

*Disadvantages of Pessimistic Locking:*

- **Reduced concurrency:** Only one transaction can access the locked data at a time.
- **Potential for deadlocks:** Multiple transactions might end up waiting on each other indefinitely.
- **Performance bottleneck** when many transactions compete for the same resources.

---

## 2. Optimistic Locking

Optimistic locking assumes that **conflicts will be rare** and that most transactions can proceed without interfering with each other. In this approach, the transaction does not lock the data immediately. Instead, it checks for conflicts only at the **time of commit**. If another transaction has modified the data since it was last read, the current transaction will be rolled back.

*Key Characteristics:*

- **Assumes minimal conflict** and doesn't lock resources initially.
- **Increases concurrency** by allowing multiple transactions to access the data at the same time.
- **Conflicts are detected at the time of update/commit**, and the transaction is rolled back if any conflict is found.
- **Requires additional checks** before the data is updated to ensure consistency.

*Example of Optimistic Locking:*

Consider the same banking system, where **Transaction 1** and **Transaction 2** are both attempting to update **Account 1**:

1. **Transaction 1** reads the balance of Account 1 and begins an update.
2. **Transaction 2** reads the balance of Account 1 and starts an update as well.

In optimistic locking, the system uses a **version number** or **timestamp** to check if the record has been modified before committing. If the version number or timestamp has changed since the data was last read, the transaction will fail to update the record.

```
-- Transaction 1
SELECT Balance, Version FROM Accounts WHERE AccountID = 1;

-- Transaction 2
SELECT Balance, Version FROM Accounts WHERE AccountID = 1;

-- Transaction 1 attempts to update
UPDATE Accounts
SET Balance = Balance - 100, Version = Version + 1
```

```
WHERE AccountID = 1 AND Version = 10;  -- Only updates if Version = 10

-- Transaction 2 attempts to update
UPDATE Accounts
SET Balance = Balance + 100, Version = Version + 1
WHERE AccountID = 1 AND Version = 10;  -- Only updates if Version = 10
```

*How It Works:*

1. **Transaction 1** retrieves the `Balance` and the `Version` number of **Account 1**.
2. **Transaction 2** retrieves the `Balance` and the `Version` number of **Account 1**.
3. **Transaction 1** updates the account's balance and increments the version number, but only if the version number has not changed.
4. **Transaction 2** tries to update the same record, but if the version number has changed since it last read the record (due to **Transaction 1**'s update), the update will fail, preventing conflicting changes.

*Advantages of Optimistic Locking:*

- **High concurrency:** Multiple transactions can access and modify different parts of the data simultaneously.
- **Better performance** when conflicts are rare, as no locks are held during the transaction.
- **Prevents unnecessary blocking** of transactions.

*Disadvantages of Optimistic Locking:*

- **Requires conflict detection** at commit time, which could lead to increased overhead.
- **May require retry logic:** If a transaction fails due to a conflict, it may need to be retried, increasing the complexity.
- Not suitable for scenarios where conflicts are frequent or consistency is critical at all times.

---

## Comparison of Optimistic and Pessimistic Locking

| Aspect | Pessimistic Locking | Optimistic Locking |
| --- | --- | --- |
| **Concurrency** | Reduces concurrency (blocks other transactions) | High concurrency (no blocking, transactions check before commit) |
| **Locking** | Locks the data as soon as it is accessed | Locks the data only at commit time if necessary |
| **Conflict Detection** | Prevents conflict by locking data | Detects conflicts at commit time |
| **Performance** | Can reduce performance (waiting for locks) | Better performance when conflicts are rare |

| Aspect | Pessimistic Locking | Optimistic Locking |
|---|---|---|
| **Use Case** | Used when conflicts are frequent and consistency is critical | Used when conflicts are rare and high throughput is needed |

---

## 1. What is a Transaction?

A **transaction** is a sequence of operations performed on a database that is treated as a single, indivisible unit. The operations either succeed as a whole (commit) or fail and have no effect (rollback).

**Example:** Transferring money between two accounts involves two operations: deducting from Account A and adding to Account B.

```
START TRANSACTION;

UPDATE Accounts SET Balance = Balance - 100 WHERE AccountID = 1;
UPDATE Accounts SET Balance = Balance + 100 WHERE AccountID = 2;

COMMIT;
```

**Output:**

- Account A: $400
- Account B: $400

If an error occurs, a `ROLLBACK` would undo both changes.

---

## 2. ACID Properties

ACID stands for **Atomicity**, **Consistency**, **Isolation**, and **Durability**. These properties ensure reliable transaction processing.

### *2.1 Atomicity*

All operations in a transaction are treated as one single unit. If one operation fails, the entire transaction is rolled back.

```
START TRANSACTION;

UPDATE Accounts SET Balance = Balance - 100 WHERE AccountID = 1;
UPDATE Accounts SET Balance = Balance + 100 WHERE AccountID = 2;
```

```
ROLLBACK;
```

**Output:**

- Account A: $500 (no change)
- Account B: $300 (no change)

### 2.2 Consistency

The database must transition from one valid state to another, ensuring no partial transactions leave the database in an inconsistent state.

Before:

- Account A: $500
- Account B: $300

After:

- Account A: $400
- Account B: $400

### 2.3 Isolation

Transactions are isolated from each other, meaning concurrent transactions do not interfere with each other.

```
START TRANSACTION;
UPDATE Accounts SET Balance = Balance - 100 WHERE AccountID = 1;
-- Transaction 1 pauses here
COMMIT;
```

### 2.4 Durability

Once a transaction is committed, its changes are permanent, even in the case of a system failure.

---

## 3. Isolation Levels

Isolation levels define the degree to which the operations in one transaction are isolated from other transactions.

### 3.1 Read Uncommitted

Transactions can read data that has not yet been committed. This allows for the highest concurrency but may lead to **dirty reads**.

```
SET TRANSACTION ISOLATION LEVEL READ UNCOMMITTED;
START TRANSACTION;
SELECT Balance FROM Accounts WHERE AccountID = 1;
```

**Output:**

- Data can be read even if another transaction is modifying the record.

### 3.2 Read Committed

A transaction can only read committed data, preventing dirty reads but allowing **non-repeatable reads**.

```
SET TRANSACTION ISOLATION LEVEL READ COMMITTED;
START TRANSACTION;
SELECT Balance FROM Accounts WHERE AccountID = 1;
```

**Output:**

- A transaction reads committed data but the value may change if another transaction commits before the current one ends.

### 3.3 Repeatable Read

Prevents both dirty reads and non-repeatable reads by ensuring that if a transaction reads a value, no other transaction can modify it until the transaction is complete.

```
SET TRANSACTION ISOLATION LEVEL REPEATABLE READ;
START TRANSACTION;
SELECT Balance FROM Accounts WHERE AccountID = 1;
-- Transaction 2 tries to update the same row but is blocked.
```

**Output:**

- Transaction 2 is blocked until Transaction 1 is completed.

### 3.4 Serializable

The highest level of isolation, where transactions are executed serially, meaning no other transaction can access the data being used.

```
SET TRANSACTION ISOLATION LEVEL SERIALIZABLE;
START TRANSACTION;
SELECT Balance FROM Accounts WHERE AccountID = 1;
```

**Output:**

- Other transactions are blocked until Transaction 1 completes, ensuring no concurrent transactions affect the results.

## 4. Handling Deadlocks

A **deadlock** occurs when two or more transactions are waiting for each other to release locks on resources, leading to a cycle of dependencies.

### 4.1 Example of Deadlock

- **Transaction 1** locks Row A and waits for Row B.
- **Transaction 2** locks Row B and waits for Row A.

```
-- Transaction 1
START TRANSACTION;
UPDATE Accounts SET Balance = Balance - 100 WHERE AccountID = 1;
-- Wait for Transaction 2 to release the lock on Row B

-- Transaction 2
START TRANSACTION;
UPDATE Accounts SET Balance = Balance - 100 WHERE AccountID = 2;
-- Wait for Transaction 1 to release the lock on Row A
```

**Resolution:** Deadlock detection will identify the circular dependency and rollback one of the transactions.

---

## 5. Optimistic vs. Pessimistic Locking

### 5.1 Pessimistic Locking

In **pessimistic locking**, locks are applied as soon as a transaction accesses data to prevent other transactions from modifying it.

```
SELECT * FROM Accounts WHERE AccountID = 1 FOR UPDATE;
-- The row is locked for the current transaction, and no other transaction
can modify it.
```

**Output:**

- **Transaction 2** is blocked from updating the same account until **Transaction 1** finishes.

### 5.2 Optimistic Locking

In **optimistic locking**, a transaction assumes there will be no conflicts and only checks for conflicts at commit time.

```
-- Transaction 1 reads the data and stores the version
SELECT Balance, Version FROM Accounts WHERE AccountID = 1;

-- Transaction 1 updates data, ensuring the version matches
```

```
UPDATE Accounts SET Balance = Balance - 100, Version = Version + 1
WHERE AccountID = 1 AND Version = 1;

-- Transaction 2 also reads and tries to update, but it will fail if version
is different.
UPDATE Accounts SET Balance = Balance + 100, Version = Version + 1
WHERE AccountID = 1 AND Version = 1;
```

**Output:**

- **Transaction 2** will fail if **Transaction 1** has already committed, preventing conflicting updates.

---

## 6. Deadlock Detection Example

Deadlock occurs when two transactions block each other while waiting for resources. The DBMS detects the deadlock and rolls back one transaction to resolve it.

```
-- Transaction 1
START TRANSACTION;
UPDATE Orders SET Status = 'Processing' WHERE OrderID = 1;

-- Transaction 2
START TRANSACTION;
UPDATE Orders SET Status = 'Shipped' WHERE OrderID = 2;

-- Deadlock occurs if both transactions try to update the same resource.
```

**Output:**

- The DBMS detects the deadlock and aborts one transaction to break the cycle.

---

## 7. Example of Isolation Level and Conflict Resolution

```
-- Transaction 1
SET TRANSACTION ISOLATION LEVEL SERIALIZABLE;
START TRANSACTION;
SELECT * FROM Accounts WHERE AccountID = 1;
-- Transaction 2 tries to modify the same account but is blocked until
Transaction 1 finishes.
```

**Output:**

- **Transaction 2** is blocked because **Transaction 1** is running in the **Serializable** isolation level.

---

## 8. Rollback Example

In case of a failure, a `ROLLBACK` will undo all the changes made during the transaction.

```
START TRANSACTION;

UPDATE Accounts SET Balance = Balance - 100 WHERE AccountID = 1;
UPDATE Accounts SET Balance = Balance + 100 WHERE AccountID = 2;

ROLLBACK;
```

**Output:**

- Account A: $500 (no change)
- Account B: $300 (no change)

---

## 9. Committing a Transaction Example

When all operations in a transaction are successful, a `COMMIT` will make the changes permanent.

```
START TRANSACTION;

UPDATE Accounts SET Balance = Balance - 100 WHERE AccountID = 1;
UPDATE Accounts SET Balance = Balance + 100 WHERE AccountID = 2;

COMMIT;
```

**Output:**

- Account A: $400
- Account B: $400

---

## 10. Transaction with Deadlock Resolution Using Timeouts

```
SET TRANSACTION ISOLATION LEVEL REPEATABLE READ;
START TRANSACTION;
UPDATE Accounts SET Balance = Balance - 100 WHERE AccountID = 1;
-- Timeout occurs and Transaction 1 is aborted.
```

**Output:**

- The transaction will be rolled back after the timeout, resolving the deadlock.

---

## 11. Deadlock Prevention using Resource Ordering

```
-- Resource Ordering
START TRANSACTION;
-- Transaction 1 locks Resource A, then Resource B
UPDATE Accounts SET Balance = Balance - 100 WHERE AccountID = 1;

START TRANSACTION;
-- Transaction 2 locks Resource B, then Resource A
UPDATE Accounts SET Balance = Balance + 100 WHERE AccountID = 2;
```

**Output:**

- Transactions are executed without deadlock due to resource ordering.

---

## 12. Optimistic Locking with Version Checking

```
SELECT Balance, Version FROM Accounts WHERE AccountID = 1;
-- Assume the version is 5
UPDATE Accounts SET Balance = Balance - 100, Version = Version + 1 WHERE
AccountID = 1 AND Version = 5;
```

**Output:**

- The transaction will fail if the version has been updated since the data was read.

---

## 13. Isolation Levels and Concurrency Control Example

```
SET TRANSACTION ISOLATION LEVEL READ COMMITTED;
START TRANSACTION;
SELECT Balance FROM Accounts WHERE AccountID = 1;
```

**Output:**

- Reads only committed data but may see different values if other transactions commit before this one completes.

---

## 14. Pessimistic Locking in Multi-User Environment

```
-- Transaction 1 locks the row
SELECT * FROM Orders WHERE OrderID = 101 FOR UPDATE;
```

```
-- Transaction 2 cannot access the locked row until Transaction 1 is
committed.
```

**Output:**

- Transaction 2 waits for Transaction 1 to release the lock.

---

## 15. Transaction Rollback on Error

```
START TRANSACTION;

UPDATE Accounts SET Balance = Balance - 100 WHERE AccountID = 1;
-- Simulate an error
UPDATE Accounts SET Balance = Balance + 100 WHERE AccountID = 2;

ROLLBACK;
```

**Output:**

- No changes are made, and the database is left in a consistent state.

## Summary

- **Pessimistic Locking** is used when conflicts are likely and data consistency must be ensured. It provides strong isolation but reduces concurrency and can lead to deadlocks.
- **Optimistic Locking** is used when conflicts are rare. It allows for higher concurrency and better performance but requires additional conflict detection mechanisms and might result in transaction rollbacks.

# CHAPTER-11

## STORED PROCEDURES AND FUNCTIONS

In SQL, **Stored Procedures** and **User-Defined Functions (UDFs)** are used to encapsulate logic and perform operations on the database. These are essential for modular, reusable, and secure database programming. Below is a detailed explanation with examples of **creating and using Stored Procedures and Functions**, **parameters**, **error handling**, and the **advantages** of using them.

---

## 1. Creating and Using Stored Procedures

A **Stored Procedure** is a set of SQL statements that can be executed as a unit. It is stored in the database and can be reused multiple times, reducing code duplication and improving maintainability.

*Creating a Stored Procedure*

```
CREATE PROCEDURE TransferMoney (
    IN FromAccount INT,
    IN ToAccount INT,
    IN Amount DECIMAL
)
BEGIN
    -- Deduct amount from FromAccount
    UPDATE Accounts
    SET Balance = Balance - Amount
    WHERE AccountID = FromAccount;

    -- Add amount to ToAccount
    UPDATE Accounts
    SET Balance = Balance + Amount
    WHERE AccountID = ToAccount;
END;
```

### Explanation:

- The procedure `TransferMoney` takes three parameters: `FromAccount`, `ToAccount`, and `Amount`.
- The procedure executes two `UPDATE` statements: one to deduct the amount from the `FromAccount` and the other to add it to the `ToAccount`.

*Using the Stored Procedure*

```
CALL TransferMoney(1, 2, 100);
```

**Explanation:**

- This will call the `TransferMoney` stored procedure, transferring 100 units from `Account 1` to `Account 2`.

---

## 2. Writing User-Defined Functions (UDFs)

A **User-Defined Function (UDF)** is similar to a stored procedure, but it is designed to return a single value, and can be used within queries like any built-in SQL function (e.g., `COUNT()`, `SUM()`, etc.).

*Creating a Simple UDF*

```
CREATE FUNCTION GetAccountBalance (AccountID INT)
RETURNS DECIMAL
BEGIN
    DECLARE Balance DECIMAL;
    SELECT Balance INTO Balance
    FROM Accounts
    WHERE AccountID = AccountID;
    RETURN Balance;
END;
```

**Explanation:**

- The function `GetAccountBalance` accepts `AccountID` as input and returns the `Balance` of the specified account.

*Using the UDF*

```
SELECT GetAccountBalance(1);
```

**Explanation:**

- This query will return the balance of `Account 1` using the `GetAccountBalance` function.

---

## 3. Parameters in Procedures and Functions

Stored Procedures and Functions can accept different types of parameters. These parameters allow for dynamic input, making procedures and functions more flexible.

*Types of Parameters:*

- **IN (Input)**: Passes values into the procedure or function.
- **OUT (Output)**: Used to return values from the procedure or function.
- **INOUT (Input/Output)**: Used to pass values in and also return values.

*Example of IN, OUT, and INOUT Parameters*

```
CREATE PROCEDURE UpdateBalance (
    IN AccountID INT,
    INOUT NewBalance DECIMAL
)
BEGIN
    -- Update the balance
    UPDATE Accounts
    SET Balance = NewBalance
    WHERE AccountID = AccountID;

    -- Get the updated balance
    SELECT Balance INTO NewBalance FROM Accounts WHERE AccountID = AccountID;
END;
```

**Explanation:**

- `AccountID` is an `IN` parameter that is used to specify which account to update.
- `NewBalance` is an `INOUT` parameter that is both input (to set the balance) and output (to return the updated balance).

*Using INOUT Parameters*

```
SET @balance = 500;
CALL UpdateBalance(1, @balance);
SELECT @balance;
```

**Explanation:**

- The balance is set to 500 before calling the procedure. After executing the procedure, the updated balance is retrieved using the `INOUT` parameter `@balance`.

---

## 4. Error Handling in Procedures

Error handling in stored procedures is important for dealing with unexpected situations like constraint violations or runtime errors. In MySQL, **`DECLARE...HANDLER`** is used for error handling.

*Error Handling Example*

```
CREATE PROCEDURE TransferMoneyWithErrorHandling (
    IN FromAccount INT,
    IN ToAccount INT,
    IN Amount DECIMAL
)
BEGIN
    DECLARE EXIT HANDLER FOR SQLEXCEPTION
    BEGIN
        -- Rollback and print an error message
        ROLLBACK;
        SELECT 'Error in transaction';
```

```
    END;

    START TRANSACTION;

    -- Deduct amount from FromAccount
    UPDATE Accounts
    SET Balance = Balance - Amount
    WHERE AccountID = FromAccount;

    -- Add amount to ToAccount
    UPDATE Accounts
    SET Balance = Balance + Amount
    WHERE AccountID = ToAccount;

    COMMIT;
END;
```

## Explanation:

- The `EXIT HANDLER` for `SQLEXCEPTION` ensures that if any SQL error occurs (e.g., insufficient balance, constraint violation), the transaction will be rolled back, and an error message will be returned.
- The `START TRANSACTION` and `COMMIT` statements ensure that both updates are executed as part of a transaction.

*Using the Procedure with Error Handling*

```
CALL TransferMoneyWithErrorHandling(1, 2, 100);
```

## Explanation:

- If any error occurs during the transfer, the transaction will be rolled back, and an error message will be shown.

---

# 5. Advantages of Stored Procedures

Stored Procedures provide several benefits, especially in complex database systems:

### *5.1 Reusability and Maintainability*

- Stored procedures can be reused across multiple applications, reducing code duplication and making maintenance easier. You can change the procedure logic without modifying the application code.

*Example:*

Instead of writing the same logic for transferring money in every application, a stored procedure can be called wherever needed.

### *5.2 Performance Optimization*

- Stored procedures are compiled and stored in the database, making them faster than running SQL queries repeatedly from applications. This reduces the overhead of query parsing, optimization, and compilation.

### *5.3 Security*

- By using stored procedures, you can control access to the underlying database tables. Instead of giving users direct access to tables, you can grant access only to stored procedures that perform specific tasks.

*Example:*

Users might be given permissions to execute the stored procedure `TransferMoney` but not to directly `UPDATE` the `Accounts` table.

### *5.4 Reduces Network Traffic*

- By grouping multiple SQL statements into a single stored procedure, you can reduce the amount of data sent over the network between the application and the database server.

---

## 1. Creating and Using Stored Procedures

**Scenario:** A procedure to transfer money between two bank accounts.

*Stored Procedure Creation*

```
CREATE PROCEDURE TransferMoney (IN FromAccount INT, IN ToAccount INT, IN
Amount DECIMAL)
BEGIN
    -- Deduct amount from FromAccount
    UPDATE Accounts
    SET Balance = Balance - Amount
    WHERE AccountID = FromAccount;

    -- Add amount to ToAccount
    UPDATE Accounts
    SET Balance = Balance + Amount
    WHERE AccountID = ToAccount;
END;
```

**Explanation:**

- This stored procedure transfers a specified amount from one account to another.

*Calling the Procedure*

```
CALL TransferMoney(1, 2, 100);
```

**Output:**

- The balance of `Account 1` will decrease by 100, and `Account 2` will increase by 100.

---

## 2. Writing User-Defined Functions (UDFs)

**Scenario:** A function to calculate the total balance in an account.

*UDF Creation*

```
CREATE FUNCTION GetAccountBalance (AccountID INT)
RETURNS DECIMAL
BEGIN
    DECLARE Balance DECIMAL;
    SELECT Balance INTO Balance
    FROM Accounts WHERE AccountID = AccountID;
    RETURN Balance;
END;
```

*Using the UDF*

```
SELECT GetAccountBalance(1);
```

**Output:**

- Returns the balance of `Account 1`.

---

## 3. Using Parameters in Procedures

**Scenario:** A stored procedure that takes multiple parameters to update an account's balance.

*Procedure with Parameters*

```
CREATE PROCEDURE UpdateAccountBalance (IN AccountID INT, IN NewBalance
DECIMAL)
BEGIN
    UPDATE Accounts
    SET Balance = NewBalance
    WHERE AccountID = AccountID;
END;
```

*Calling the Procedure*

```
CALL UpdateAccountBalance(1, 500);
```

**Output:**

- Updates the balance of `Account 1` to 500.

## 4. Using INOUT Parameters

**Scenario:** A stored procedure to adjust and return the updated balance using `INOUT` parameters.

*Procedure with INOUT Parameter*

```
CREATE PROCEDURE AdjustBalance (INOUT AccountID INT, INOUT Balance DECIMAL)
BEGIN
    -- Deducting $50 from the account balance
    SET Balance = Balance - 50;
    UPDATE Accounts
    SET Balance = Balance
    WHERE AccountID = AccountID;
END;
```

*Using INOUT Parameter*

```
SET @balance = 200;
SET @id = 1;
CALL AdjustBalance(@id, @balance);
SELECT @balance;
```

**Output:**

- After calling the procedure, the balance of `Account 1` is reduced by 50, and the updated balance is returned.

---

## 5. Error Handling in Procedures

**Scenario:** A procedure that transfers money between accounts, with error handling for any failure.

*Procedure with Error Handling*

```
CREATE PROCEDURE TransferMoneyWithErrorHandling (IN FromAccount INT, IN
ToAccount INT, IN Amount DECIMAL)
BEGIN
    DECLARE EXIT HANDLER FOR SQLEXCEPTION
    BEGIN
        ROLLBACK;
        SELECT 'Transaction Failed';
    END;

    START TRANSACTION;

    -- Deduct from FromAccount
    UPDATE Accounts SET Balance = Balance - Amount WHERE AccountID =
FromAccount;
```

```
    -- Add to ToAccount
    UPDATE Accounts SET Balance = Balance + Amount WHERE AccountID =
ToAccount;

    COMMIT;
END;
```

*Calling the Procedure*

```
CALL TransferMoneyWithErrorHandling(1, 2, 100);
```

**Output:**

- If any SQL exception occurs, the transaction will be rolled back, and an error message "Transaction Failed" will be displayed.

---

## 6. Returning Values Using Functions

**Scenario:** A function that calculates the balance difference between two accounts.

*UDF Creation*

```
CREATE FUNCTION BalanceDifference (AccountID1 INT, AccountID2 INT)
RETURNS DECIMAL
BEGIN
    DECLARE Balance1 DECIMAL;
    DECLARE Balance2 DECIMAL;

    SELECT Balance INTO Balance1 FROM Accounts WHERE AccountID = AccountID1;
    SELECT Balance INTO Balance2 FROM Accounts WHERE AccountID = AccountID2;

    RETURN Balance1 - Balance2;
END;
```

*Calling the Function*

```
SELECT BalanceDifference(1, 2);
```

**Output:**

- Returns the difference in balance between `Account 1` and `Account 2`.

---

## 7. Advantages of Stored Procedures: Performance Optimization

**Scenario:** A stored procedure reduces the need for multiple round trips to the database.

*Procedure for Multiple Actions*

```
CREATE PROCEDURE UpdateAccountInfo (IN AccountID INT, IN Name VARCHAR(100),
IN Balance DECIMAL)
BEGIN
    UPDATE Accounts
```

```sql
    SET Name = Name, Balance = Balance
    WHERE AccountID = AccountID;

    SELECT * FROM Accounts WHERE AccountID = AccountID;
END;
```

*Calling the Procedure*

```sql
CALL UpdateAccountInfo(1, 'John Doe', 1200);
```

**Output:**

- Updates the account and returns the updated record in one round trip.

---

## 8. Using a Function for Conditional Logic

**Scenario:** A function that checks if an account balance is sufficient to perform a transaction.

*UDF Creation*

```sql
CREATE FUNCTION IsBalanceSufficient (AccountID INT, Amount DECIMAL)
RETURNS BOOLEAN
BEGIN
    DECLARE CurrentBalance DECIMAL;
    SELECT Balance INTO CurrentBalance FROM Accounts WHERE AccountID =
AccountID;

    RETURN IF(CurrentBalance >= Amount, TRUE, FALSE);
END;
```

*Calling the Function*

```sql
SELECT IsBalanceSufficient(1, 500);
```

**Output:**

- Returns `TRUE` if the balance in `Account 1` is sufficient for the transaction.

---

## 9. Using Error Handling in a Function

**Scenario:** A function that returns an error message if the account is not found.

*Function with Error Handling*

```sql
CREATE FUNCTION GetAccountBalanceWithErrorHandling (AccountID INT)
RETURNS DECIMAL
BEGIN
    DECLARE Balance DECIMAL DEFAULT -1;

    BEGIN
        SELECT Balance INTO Balance FROM Accounts WHERE AccountID =
AccountID;
```

```
        IF Balance IS NULL THEN
            SIGNAL SQLSTATE '45000' SET MESSAGE_TEXT = 'Account not found';
        END IF;
    END;

    RETURN Balance;
END;
```

*Calling the Function*

```
SELECT GetAccountBalanceWithErrorHandling(10);
```

**Output:**

- If the account is not found, an error message "Account not found" will be raised.

---

## 10. Security Benefits of Stored Procedures

**Scenario:** Granting users access only to procedures without direct access to underlying tables.

*Granting Permissions*

```
GRANT EXECUTE ON PROCEDURE TransferMoney TO UserName;
```

**Explanation:**

- This allows `UserName` to execute the `TransferMoney` stored procedure but does not grant access to directly modify the `Accounts` table.

**Output:**

- The user can execute the procedure but cannot directly update or query the `Accounts` table.

## Conclusion

Stored Procedures and Functions offer a powerful way to encapsulate logic in the database, improving code reusability, performance, and security. By properly using parameters and handling errors, we can make database operations more robust and efficient. Understanding how to implement these tools will help you optimize your database management practices.

# CHAPTER-12

## INTERVIEW-FOCUSED PROBLEM SOLVING

SQL challenges in interviews typically test your ability to write efficient queries, handle complex data relationships, and solve real-world problems using SQL. Here are some common challenges you might face during an SQL interview:

---

### 1. SQL Joins

SQL Joins are used to combine data from two or more tables based on a related column. When working with multiple tables, you often need to retrieve data from each table that shares a common key, such as a foreign key. SQL supports several types of joins, and each serves different purposes in retrieving data.

Let's explore **Inner Join**, one of the most commonly used joins, and see how it works with an example.

---

### Scenario: Find All Customers Who Have Placed an Order

*Problem:*

You have two tables, `Customers` and `Orders`. You want to find all the customers who have placed at least one order.

- **Customers Table:**

| CustomerID | Name |
|---|---|
| 1 | John Smith |
| 2 | Jane Doe |
| 3 | Bob Brown |
| 4 | Alice Green |

- **Orders Table:**

| OrderID | CustomerID | Amount |
|---|---|---|
| 101 | 1 | 500.00 |
| 102 | 2 | 300.00 |
| 103 | 1 | 150.00 |
| 104 | 3 | 200.00 |

*Solution Using JOIN:*

We use an **INNER JOIN** to retrieve the customers who have placed an order. An inner join returns only the rows that have matching values in both tables.

```
SELECT c.CustomerID, c.Name, o.OrderID
FROM Customers c
JOIN Orders o ON c.CustomerID = o.CustomerID;
```

## Explanation:

- `JOIN` is used to combine the `Customers` and `Orders` tables.
- `c.CustomerID = o.CustomerID` specifies the condition to join the tables, meaning we are looking for rows in the `Customers` table where the `CustomerID` matches the `CustomerID` in the `Orders` table.
- The `SELECT` clause specifies the columns to retrieve: `CustomerID`, `Name`, and `OrderID`.
- The result will give a list of customers who have placed an order, along with their corresponding `OrderID`.

*Output:*

| CustomerID | Name | OrderID |
|---|---|---|
| 1 | John Smith | 101 |
| 1 | John Smith | 103 |
| 2 | Jane Doe | 102 |
| 3 | Bob Brown | 104 |

## Explanation of the Output:

- John Smith placed two orders (Order 101 and Order 103).
- Jane Doe placed one order (Order 102).
- Bob Brown placed one order (Order 104).
- Alice Green does not appear in the result because she has not placed any orders.

## Other Types of SQL Joins

SQL supports several types of joins, each designed to handle different scenarios:

---

## 2. LEFT JOIN (or LEFT OUTER JOIN)

A **LEFT JOIN** returns all rows from the left table (the table before `JOIN`), and the matched rows from the right table. If there's no match, the result is `NULL` from the right table.

*Scenario: Find all customers and their orders (including customers who have not placed any orders).*

```
SELECT c.CustomerID, c.Name, o.OrderID
FROM Customers c
LEFT JOIN Orders o ON c.CustomerID = o.CustomerID;
```

*Output:*

| CustomerID | Name | OrderID |
|---|---|---|
| 1 | John Smith | 101 |
| 1 | John Smith | 103 |
| 2 | Jane Doe | 102 |
| 3 | Bob Brown | 104 |
| 4 | Alice Green | NULL |

### Explanation:

- All customers are shown in the result.
- Alice Green does not have any orders, so her `OrderID` is `NULL`.

---

## 3. RIGHT JOIN (or RIGHT OUTER JOIN)

A **RIGHT JOIN** returns all rows from the right table (the table after `JOIN`), and the matched rows from the left table. If there's no match, the result is `NULL` from the left table.

*Scenario: Find all orders and the corresponding customers, including orders that don't have a matching customer (though rare in a well-designed database).*

```
SELECT c.CustomerID, c.Name, o.OrderID
FROM Customers c
RIGHT JOIN Orders o ON c.CustomerID = o.CustomerID;
```

*Output:*

| CustomerID | Name | OrderID |
|---|---|---|
| 1 | John Smith | 101 |
| 1 | John Smith | 103 |
| 2 | Jane Doe | 102 |
| 3 | Bob Brown | 104 |

**Explanation:**

- Right joins are less commonly used in this case since every order is expected to have a customer.
- If there were any orders with no customers, they would be shown with `NULL` for `CustomerID` and `Name`.

---

## 4. FULL JOIN (or FULL OUTER JOIN)

A **FULL JOIN** returns all rows when there is a match in either the left or right table. If there's no match, the result is `NULL` from the missing side.

*Scenario: Find all customers and all orders, even if there are customers with no orders and orders with no customers.*

```
SELECT c.CustomerID, c.Name, o.OrderID
FROM Customers c
FULL OUTER JOIN Orders o ON c.CustomerID = o.CustomerID;
```

*Output:*

| CustomerID | Name | OrderID |
|---|---|---|
| 1 | John Smith | 101 |
| 1 | John Smith | 103 |
| 2 | Jane Doe | 102 |
| 3 | Bob Brown | 104 |
| 4 | Alice Green | NULL |

**Explanation:**

- The result includes all customers and orders, and it returns `NULL` when there is no match on either side.

## 5. SELF JOIN

A **SELF JOIN** is a regular join but the table is joined with itself. This is useful when comparing rows within the same table.

*Scenario: Find all employees and their managers (where the manager is also an employee).*

Assume you have an `Employees` table with columns `EmployeeID`, `Name`, and `ManagerID`.

```
SELECT e.Name AS Employee, m.Name AS Manager
FROM Employees e
LEFT JOIN Employees m ON e.ManagerID = m.EmployeeID;
```

*Explanation:*

- `e` is an alias for employees.
- `m` is an alias for managers (the same `Employees` table).
- This join allows us to pair employees with their managers.

---

## Conclusion

SQL Joins are essential tools for retrieving related data from multiple tables. By using **INNER JOIN**, **LEFT JOIN**, **RIGHT JOIN**, **FULL JOIN**, and **SELF JOIN**, you can effectively combine data and extract meaningful insights from relational databases. Understanding when and how to use each type of join is a crucial skill for solving complex SQL problems, especially in interviews.

---

## 2. Subqueries

A **subquery** is a query nested inside another query, typically used to retrieve values that are used by the outer query. Subqueries can be used in the `SELECT`, `FROM`, `WHERE`, or `HAVING` clauses of a SQL query.

### Scenario: Get the Names of Employees Who Earn More Than the Average Salary in Their Department

In this scenario, the goal is to retrieve the names of employees whose salary is higher than the average salary of their respective department. A **subquery** is used here to calculate the average salary for each department, which is then compared against the employee's salary in the main query.

---

## Database Structure:

Assume the following structure for the `Employees` table:

| EmployeeID | Name | Salary | DepartmentID |
|---|---|---|---|
| 1 | John Smith | 70000 | 1 |
| 2 | Jane Doe | 80000 | 1 |
| 3 | Bob Brown | 60000 | 2 |
| 4 | Alice Green | 75000 | 2 |
| 5 | Tom White | 90000 | 3 |
| 6 | Sarah Black | 95000 | 3 |

Here, the task is to get the names of employees whose salary is **greater than the average salary** in their respective department.

---

## Solution Using Subquery

*SQL Query:*

```
SELECT Name
FROM Employees
WHERE Salary > (
    SELECT AVG(Salary)
    FROM Employees
    WHERE DepartmentID = Employees.DepartmentID
);
```

*Explanation of the Query:*

1. **Main Query**:
   - `SELECT Name FROM Employees`: This selects the `Name` column from the `Employees` table.
2. **Subquery**:
   - `(SELECT AVG(Salary) FROM Employees WHERE DepartmentID = Employees.DepartmentID)`: This subquery calculates the average salary for each department. The `DepartmentID = Employees.DepartmentID` condition ensures that the average salary is calculated specifically for each department.
3. **Comparison**:
   - `WHERE Salary >`: The outer query checks if the salary of each employee is greater than the average salary of their respective department, which is provided by the subquery.

*Step-by-Step Execution:*

1. **For Department 1 (DepartmentID = 1):**
   - The **average salary** is `(70000 + 80000) / 2 = 75000`.
   - The query checks for employees whose **salary is greater than 75000**.
   - **Result**: `Jane Doe` has a salary of 80000, which is greater than 75000.
2. **For Department 2 (DepartmentID = 2):**
   - The **average salary** is `(60000 + 75000) / 2 = 67500`.
   - The query checks for employees whose **salary is greater than 67500**.
   - **Result**: `Alice Green` has a salary of 75000, which is greater than 67500.
3. **For Department 3 (DepartmentID = 3):**
   - The **average salary** is `(90000 + 95000) / 2 = 92500`.
   - The query checks for employees whose **salary is greater than 92500**.
   - **Result**: `Sarah Black` has a salary of 95000, which is greater than 92500.

*Final Result:*

| Name |
|---|
| Jane Doe |
| Alice Green |
| Sarah Black |

---

## How Subqueries Work in This Context:

- The subquery `(SELECT AVG(Salary) FROM Employees WHERE DepartmentID = Employees.DepartmentID)` calculates the average salary for the department of each employee.
- The main query compares the `Salary` of each employee against the **average salary of their department**.
- This ensures that only employees who earn **more than the average salary in their respective department** are included in the result.

---

## Advantages of Using Subqueries:

1. **Clarity and Simplicity**: Subqueries make complex conditions easier to write and understand by breaking them into smaller, manageable parts.
2. **Dynamic Comparison**: Subqueries allow dynamic calculations (like averages or totals) to be used directly in the outer query.
3. **Data Filtering**: Subqueries can be used to filter data based on complex criteria, such as finding records that match a calculated value (e.g., salary > department's average salary).

## Alternative Approach Without Subquery:

Another way to solve this problem without using a subquery is to use **joins**. We can calculate the average salary by joining the `Employees` table with a derived table that contains the average salary per department.

*SQL Query Using JOIN:*

```
SELECT e.Name
FROM Employees e
JOIN (
    SELECT DepartmentID, AVG(Salary) AS AvgSalary
    FROM Employees
    GROUP BY DepartmentID
) avg_dept_salary ON e.DepartmentID = avg_dept_salary.DepartmentID
WHERE e.Salary > avg_dept_salary.AvgSalary;
```

*Explanation of the JOIN Approach:*

1. The subquery `(SELECT DepartmentID, AVG(Salary) AS AvgSalary FROM Employees GROUP BY DepartmentID)` calculates the average salary for each department.
2. We then **JOIN** this result with the original `Employees` table on `DepartmentID` to match each employee to their department's average salary.
3. The `WHERE e.Salary > avg_dept_salary.AvgSalary` condition ensures that only employees who earn more than the average salary of their department are selected.

---

## Output of the JOIN Approach:

| Name |
|---|
| Jane Doe |
| Alice Green |
| Sarah Black |

---

## Conclusion:

- **Subquery Approach**: The subquery efficiently calculates the department-wise average salary and compares it against each employee's salary.
- **JOIN Approach**: The JOIN method achieves the same result, but might be more efficient in cases of larger datasets or more complex queries.

Both approaches have their use cases, and understanding when to use a subquery versus a JOIN is essential for writing efficient SQL queries.

### 3. Aggregation and Grouping

Aggregation and grouping are essential concepts in SQL for summarizing data. They help in performing operations like counting, summing, averaging, etc., over groups of rows that share a common attribute.

*Scenario: Find the Total Number of Orders Placed by Each Customer*

In this scenario, we want to retrieve the total number of orders placed by each customer from the `Orders` table. To achieve this, we will use SQL's **GROUP BY** clause along with the **COUNT()** aggregate function.

---

### Database Structure:

Assume we have the following `Orders` table:

| OrderID | CustomerID | OrderDate |
|---|---|---|
| 1 | 101 | 2024-01-10 |
| 2 | 102 | 2024-01-12 |
| 3 | 101 | 2024-01-15 |
| 4 | 103 | 2024-01-16 |
| 5 | 101 | 2024-01-20 |
| 6 | 102 | 2024-01-22 |

---

### SQL Query to Find Total Orders per Customer:

```
ELECT CustomerID, COUNT(OrderID) AS TotalOrders
FROM Orders
GROUP BY CustomerID;
```

---

## Explanation of the Query:

1. **SELECT Clause**:
   - `SELECT CustomerID, COUNT(OrderID) AS TotalOrders`: This part of the query selects the `CustomerID` from the `Orders` table and calculates the **total number of orders** for each customer using the `COUNT(OrderID)` function. The `AS TotalOrders` part renames the result of the count as `TotalOrders` for clarity.
2. **FROM Clause**:
   - `FROM Orders`: This specifies that we are working with the `Orders` table.
3. **GROUP BY Clause**:
   - `GROUP BY CustomerID`: The `GROUP BY` clause is used to group the rows based on the `CustomerID` column. This means that all orders with the same `CustomerID` will be grouped together, and the aggregation function (`COUNT`) will operate on these groups.
4. **COUNT() Function**:
   - `COUNT(OrderID)`: This aggregate function counts the number of `OrderID` entries for each customer. The result will give the total number of orders for each `CustomerID`.

---

## Step-by-Step Execution:

1. **CustomerID = 101**:
   - Orders: 1, 3, 5
   - Total Orders: 3
2. **CustomerID = 102**:
   - Orders: 2, 6
   - Total Orders: 2
3. **CustomerID = 103**:
   - Orders: 4
   - Total Orders: 1

---

## Result:

The query will return the following result:

| CustomerID | TotalOrders |
|---|---|
| 101 | 3 |
| 102 | 2 |
| 103 | 1 |

---

## Explanation of Aggregation Functions:

- **COUNT()**: This function counts the number of rows or non-NULL values in a specific column. It is commonly used when you need to count occurrences of a certain attribute (e.g., number of orders, number of customers).
    - Example: `COUNT(OrderID)` counts how many orders each customer has placed.
- **SUM()**: This function calculates the total sum of values in a numeric column.
    - Example: `SUM(OrderAmount)` would return the total order value for each customer.
- **AVG()**: This function calculates the average of a numeric column.
    - Example: `AVG(OrderAmount)` would return the average order amount for each customer.
- **MIN()**: This function returns the minimum value in a column.
    - Example: `MIN(OrderAmount)` would return the smallest order value for each customer.
- **MAX()**: This function returns the maximum value in a column.
    - Example: `MAX(OrderAmount)` would return the largest order value for each customer.

---

## Additional Examples of Grouping and Aggregation:

*1. Find the Total Order Value for Each Customer*

If we wanted to find the total amount spent by each customer, we could use the **SUM()** function to sum the order values.

```
SELECT CustomerID, SUM(OrderAmount) AS TotalSpent
FROM Orders
GROUP BY CustomerID;
```

- This will sum the `OrderAmount` for each customer and return the total spent by each customer.

*2. Find the Average Order Value per Customer*

```
SELECT CustomerID, AVG(OrderAmount) AS AvgOrderValue
FROM Orders
GROUP BY CustomerID;
```

- This query will calculate the average order amount per customer.

*3. Find the Highest and Lowest Order Values per Customer*

```
SELECT CustomerID, MAX(OrderAmount) AS MaxOrderValue, MIN(OrderAmount) AS
MinOrderValue
FROM Orders
GROUP BY CustomerID;
```

- This query uses both the **MAX()** and **MIN()** functions to find the highest and lowest order values placed by each customer.

---

## Complex Example: Find Customers Who Have Placed More Than 2 Orders

To find customers who have placed more than two orders, we can combine **GROUP BY** with the **HAVING** clause.

```
SELECT CustomerID, COUNT(OrderID) AS TotalOrders
FROM Orders
GROUP BY CustomerID
HAVING COUNT(OrderID) > 2;
```

- The `HAVING` clause filters groups after the aggregation is performed. In this case, it filters out any customers who have placed two or fewer orders.

*Explanation:*

- `HAVING COUNT(OrderID) > 2`: This condition filters groups (customers) whose total order count is greater than 2.

---

## Key Points to Remember:

1. **GROUP BY**: This clause groups the result set by one or more columns (in this case, `CustomerID`), so that aggregate functions can be applied to each group.
2. **HAVING**: Used to filter groups based on conditions applied to aggregate functions. Unlike `WHERE`, which filters rows before grouping, `HAVING` filters groups after the grouping is done.
3. **Aggregate Functions**: Functions like `COUNT()`, `SUM()`, `AVG()`, `MIN()`, and `MAX()` are used to perform calculations on groups of rows.
4. **Efficiency**: Using `GROUP BY` can be more efficient than using subqueries, especially when dealing with large datasets, as the grouping and aggregation are done in a single pass over the data.

---

## Conclusion:

**Aggregation and Grouping** are powerful tools in SQL for summarizing and analyzing data. By using functions like `COUNT()`, `SUM()`, `AVG()`, and others in combination with `GROUP BY`, you can answer a wide range of analytical questions. The ability to group data by specific columns and apply aggregate functions is essential for tasks like generating reports and summarizing large datasets.

---

## 4. Handling Duplicates

Handling duplicates is a common task in SQL, especially when dealing with large datasets where duplicate records may appear due to data entry, joins, or other factors. In SQL, the **DISTINCT** keyword is used to eliminate duplicate rows from the result set and return only unique values.

Let's go through a detailed explanation with an example to understand how to handle duplicates effectively.

---

### Scenario: Retrieve a List of Unique Product Names Ordered by Customers

In this scenario, we want to retrieve a unique list of product names that have been ordered by customers from the `Orders` table. The table may contain multiple entries for the same product name if multiple customers have ordered it, so we need to ensure that we get each product name only once.

---

### Database Structure:

Assume we have the following `Orders` table:

| OrderID | CustomerID | ProductName | OrderDate |
|---|---|---|---|
| 1 | 101 | Laptop | 2024-01-10 |
| 2 | 102 | Smartphone | 2024-01-12 |
| 3 | 101 | Laptop | 2024-01-15 |
| 4 | 103 | Tablet | 2024-01-16 |
| 5 | 102 | Laptop | 2024-01-20 |
| 6 | 103 | Smartphone | 2024-01-22 |

---

### SQL Query to Retrieve Unique Product Names:

```
SELECT DISTINCT ProductName
FROM Orders;
```

---

### Explanation of the Query:

1. **SELECT Clause**:
    - `SELECT DISTINCT ProductName`: This part of the query selects the `ProductName` column, but the keyword `DISTINCT` ensures that only unique product names are returned in the result. Any duplicate product names (e.g., 'Laptop' in this case) will be removed from the final result.
2. **FROM Clause**:
    - `FROM Orders`: Specifies that we are retrieving data from the `Orders` table.

---

## Step-by-Step Execution:

1. The `DISTINCT` keyword checks the `ProductName` column for duplicate entries. It will return only one instance of each product name, even if it appears multiple times in the `Orders` table.
2. The query will eliminate the duplicate `ProductName` values and return a unique list of product names.

---

## Result:

The result of the query will be:

| ProductName |
|---|
| Laptop |
| Smartphone |
| Tablet |

- Here, the `Laptop` and `Smartphone` names appear multiple times in the `Orders` table, but the `DISTINCT` keyword ensures that they are listed only once.

---

## Why Use DISTINCT?

- **Avoiding Redundancy**: When you need to remove duplicates from the result set, `DISTINCT` is a convenient and simple method to return only unique rows.
- **Improved Data Analysis**: It helps when analyzing data by ensuring that only unique values are considered, such as when analyzing the diversity of products ordered or customers served.

---

## Other Common Scenarios with DISTINCT

*1. Retrieve Unique Customer IDs Who Have Placed Orders:*

To find all customers who have placed an order, we would use the `DISTINCT` keyword on the `CustomerID` column.

```
SELECT DISTINCT CustomerID
FROM Orders;
```

- This will return a list of unique customer IDs who have placed orders, eliminating any duplicate `CustomerID` values.

*2. Retrieve Unique Combinations of Product and Customer:*

If you need to find all unique pairs of products ordered by customers, you can combine `DISTINCT` with multiple columns.

```
SELECT DISTINCT CustomerID, ProductName
FROM Orders;
```

- This will return unique combinations of `CustomerID` and `ProductName`, ensuring that each customer-product pair is listed only once, even if a customer has ordered the same product multiple times.

---

## DISTINCT with Aggregate Functions:

You can also use `DISTINCT` with aggregate functions like `COUNT()`, `SUM()`, or `AVG()` to perform operations on unique values.

*1. Count Unique Product Names Ordered by Customers:*

To count how many unique products have been ordered, you can use `COUNT()` with `DISTINCT`.

```
SELECT COUNT(DISTINCT ProductName) AS UniqueProductCount
FROM Orders;
```

- This query counts the number of distinct product names in the `Orders` table.

*2. Find the Total Number of Unique Customers Who Have Ordered a Product:*

```
SELECT COUNT(DISTINCT CustomerID) AS UniqueCustomers
FROM Orders
WHERE ProductName = 'Laptop';
```

- This query returns the total number of unique customers who have ordered the product 'Laptop'.

---

## Considerations When Using DISTINCT:

1. **Performance**: Using `DISTINCT` may impact query performance, especially on large datasets, as the database has to check all rows and remove duplicates. It's important to use `DISTINCT` only when necessary.
2. **Avoid Overuse**: While `DISTINCT` is useful, overusing it in queries with multiple joins or on large tables can lead to slower performance. In some cases, restructuring the query or optimizing the database schema might be a better approach.
3. **DISTINCT on Multiple Columns**: You can use `DISTINCT` on multiple columns, and it will return unique combinations of values across those columns. However, be cautious when applying `DISTINCT` to multiple columns as it might lead to unexpected results or performance issues.

---

## Example of DISTINCT with Multiple Columns:

```
SELECT DISTINCT CustomerID, ProductName
FROM Orders;
```

- This query will return unique pairs of `CustomerID` and `ProductName`, meaning if a customer orders the same product multiple times, it will only be counted once.

---

## Conclusion:

The **DISTINCT** keyword is a powerful tool for handling duplicates in SQL. It allows you to retrieve unique values from a column or combination of columns, ensuring that duplicate data does not appear in the query result. Understanding when and how to use `DISTINCT` effectively is crucial for data analysis, reporting, and optimizing SQL queries for performance.

---

## 5. Window Functions

**Scenario:** Retrieve the salary of each employee along with the average salary in their department.

*Solution Using Window Functions*

```
SELECT Name, Salary, AVG(Salary) OVER (PARTITION BY DepartmentID) AS
DepartmentAvgSalary
FROM Employees;
```

**Explanation:**

- This example uses the **AVG()** window function with the **PARTITION BY** clause to compute the average salary of each department while retaining the individual employee's salary in the result set.

---

## Problem-Solving Strategies for SQL Interviews

When faced with SQL challenges in interviews, it's essential to follow a structured approach to solve problems:

---

### 1. Understand the Problem

Before jumping into writing queries, make sure you fully understand the problem. Break it down into smaller, manageable parts:

- **Entities:** What are the main tables or entities involved?
- **Relationships:** What relationships exist between the tables?
- **Conditions:** What filters need to be applied (WHERE clause)?
- **Expected Output:** What data is expected as the result?

---

### 2. Plan Your Query

Once you understand the problem, plan your approach:

- **Identify Required Data:** Which columns and tables do you need?
- **Choose the Right SQL Clauses:** Decide if you need `JOIN`, `GROUP BY`, `ORDER BY`, or subqueries.
- **Consider Performance:** Think about using indexes or filtering data early in your query to improve performance.

---

### 3. Write and Test Incrementally

Start writing the query step by step:

- Begin with basic parts (like `SELECT` and `FROM`).
- Add more complexity gradually (like `JOIN`, `GROUP BY`).
- Test each part to ensure correctness and optimize as you go.

---

## Writing Efficient and Scalable Queries

**Scenario:** Retrieve the top 10 products by sales from a large `Sales` table.

*Inefficient Query (Full Table Scan)*

```
SELECT ProductID, SUM(Amount) AS TotalSales
FROM Sales
GROUP BY ProductID
ORDER BY TotalSales DESC
LIMIT 10;
```

**Explanation:**

- This query can be inefficient if the `Sales` table is large because it may require scanning the entire table.

*Optimized Query (Using Index)*

```
CREATE INDEX idx_sales_productid ON Sales(ProductID);
SELECT ProductID, SUM(Amount) AS TotalSales
FROM Sales
GROUP BY ProductID
ORDER BY TotalSales DESC
LIMIT 10;
```

**Explanation:**

- Creating an index on the `ProductID` column speeds up the query by allowing the database to locate relevant data more quickly.

---

## Debugging and Optimizing SQL Code

**Scenario:** A query that's running slowly due to a large dataset.

*Original Query:*

```
SELECT ProductID, SUM(Amount)
FROM Sales
WHERE Date >= '2023-01-01'
GROUP BY ProductID;
```

*Optimization Steps*

1. **Examine Execution Plan:**
   - Use `EXPLAIN` to analyze how the query is being executed:

```
EXPLAIN SELECT ProductID, SUM(Amount) FROM Sales WHERE Date >= '2023-
01-01' GROUP BY ProductID;
```

   - This can help identify performance bottlenecks, such as full table scans or missing indexes.
2. **Optimize Filters:**
   - Ensure the date filter `WHERE Date >= '2023-01-01'` is using an index if possible.
3. **Create Indexes:**

```
CREATE INDEX idx_sales_date ON Sales(Date);
```

   **Explanation:**

   - Creating an index on the `Date` column can improve query performance by reducing the number of rows scanned.

---

## Time-Bound Query Writing Exercises

In SQL interviews, time-bound exercises are often used to test how quickly and efficiently you can write queries under pressure. Here's an example with a 5-minute time limit.

---

## Scenario: Find the top 5 products by sales in the last 6 months.

*Solution:*

1. **Identify Key Information:**
   - The table involved is `Sales`.
   - We need to filter data for the last 6 months.
   - We need to find the top 5 products by sales amount.
2. **Write the Query:**

```
SELECT ProductID, SUM(Amount) AS TotalSales
FROM Sales
WHERE Date >= CURDATE() - INTERVAL 6 MONTH
GROUP BY ProductID
ORDER BY TotalSales DESC
LIMIT 5;
```

**Explanation:**

- The query uses `CURDATE() - INTERVAL 6 MONTH` to filter sales data for the last 6 months.
- We then use `GROUP BY` and `ORDER BY` to sum sales by product and sort them by total sales in descending order.

**Output:**

- This query will return the top 5 products by total sales in the last 6 months.

---

## Conclusion

When tackling SQL challenges in interviews, it's essential to follow a structured approach: understand the problem, break it down, and write optimized, scalable queries. By practicing various SQL challenges, understanding performance optimization, and debugging efficiently, you can improve your query-writing skills and succeed in interviews. Time-bound exercises test not only your SQL knowledge but also your ability to think under pressure, making them an essential part of preparation.

# CHAPTER-13

## COMMON SQL INTERVIEW QUESTIONS AND SOLUTIONS

SQL (Structured Query Language) is a crucial skill for developers, analysts, and engineers. SQL interview questions can vary in complexity, ranging from basic queries to real-life scenarios requiring optimization skills. Below, we'll walk through some common SQL interview questions, their solutions, and the reasoning behind them.

---

**1.** SQL (Structured Query Language) is the standard language for managing and manipulating relational databases. Below are explanations for some basic SQL questions, complete with examples to illustrate how these concepts work.

---

### Q1. What is SQL?

**Answer:** SQL (Structured Query Language) is a domain-specific language designed for managing and manipulating relational databases. It provides commands for querying, inserting, updating, and deleting data in a database. SQL also allows you to create and modify the structure of database objects such as tables, indexes, and views. It is widely used in database systems like MySQL, PostgreSQL, Oracle, SQL Server, etc.

**Key Uses of SQL:**

- **Querying data**: Retrieving specific information from the database (e.g., `SELECT` queries).
- **Inserting data**: Adding new records to a table (e.g., `INSERT INTO`).
- **Updating data**: Modifying existing records (e.g., `UPDATE`).
- **Deleting data**: Removing records from a table (e.g., `DELETE`).
- **Defining schema**: Creating and modifying the structure of database objects (e.g., `CREATE TABLE`, `ALTER TABLE`).
- **Controlling access**: Managing database permissions and security (e.g., `GRANT`, `REVOKE`).

---

### Q2. What is a Primary Key in SQL?

**Answer:** A **Primary Key** is a column (or a combination of columns) in a table that uniquely identifies each record in that table. A primary key must satisfy the following constraints:

- **Uniqueness**: No two rows can have the same value for the primary key.
- **Non-nullability**: A primary key column cannot have `NULL` values. Every record must have a valid value for the primary key.

**Example:**

Let's consider a table called `Employees`:

```
CREATE TABLE Employees (
    EmployeeID INT PRIMARY KEY,
    Name VARCHAR(100),
    Salary DECIMAL(10, 2),
    DepartmentID INT
);
```

In this table, `EmployeeID` is the primary key, which uniquely identifies each employee.

**Explanation:**

- Each employee must have a unique `EmployeeID`, and it cannot be NULL. This ensures that no two employees can have the same ID, and every employee record will have a valid identifier.

---

## Q3. Write a SQL query to find the second-highest salary from the Employees table.

**Solution:**

```
SELECT MAX(Salary) AS SecondHighestSalary
FROM Employees
WHERE Salary < (SELECT MAX(Salary) FROM Employees);
```

**Explanation:**

1. **Subquery**: The subquery `(SELECT MAX(Salary) FROM Employees)` retrieves the highest salary from the `Employees` table.
2. **Main Query**: The main query selects the maximum salary that is less than the highest salary, which will give us the second-highest salary.

Here's how the query works:

- First, we calculate the highest salary in the `Employees` table using the `MAX(Salary)` function.
- Then, we use a `WHERE` clause to filter out any salary equal to the highest salary by using the condition `Salary < (SELECT MAX(Salary)...)`.
- Finally, the `MAX(Salary)` in the outer query returns the highest salary from the remaining records, which is the second-highest overall.

**Example:**

Consider the `Employees` table:

| EmployeeID | Name | Salary |
|---|---|---|
| 1 | John | 5000 |
| 2 | Jane | 7000 |
| 3 | Alice | 8000 |
| 4 | Bob | 6000 |

- The highest salary is `8000` (Alice).
- The second-highest salary is `7000` (Jane).

The query will return:

| SecondHighestSalary |
|---|
| 7000 |

---

## Summary of the Concepts

1. **SQL** is a language used to communicate with relational databases for tasks like querying, updating, inserting, and managing data.
2. A **Primary Key** is a column that uniquely identifies records in a table and must not allow `NULL` values.
3. To find the **second-highest salary**, a query can use a subquery to find the highest salary, and then filter to find the maximum salary that is lower than the highest.

---

These basic SQL concepts form the foundation of working with databases and are commonly asked in SQL-related interviews for roles involving database management and data manipulation.

---

## 2. Intermediate SQL Scenarios

Here are three common intermediate-level SQL scenarios along with detailed explanations and examples to demonstrate their solutions.

## Q1. Write a query to get the number of employees in each department.

**Solution:**

```
SELECT DepartmentID, COUNT(EmployeeID) AS EmployeeCount
FROM Employees
GROUP BY DepartmentID;
```

**Explanation:**

- **COUNT(EmployeeID)**: This counts the number of employees (rows) in each department. The `COUNT()` function is an aggregate function that returns the number of rows that match a given condition.
- **GROUP BY DepartmentID**: This groups the result set by the `DepartmentID` column. For each department, the query counts the employees (based on `EmployeeID`) and returns the result for each department separately.

**Example:**

Consider the `Employees` table:

| EmployeeID | Name | DepartmentID | Salary |
|---|---|---|---|
| 1 | John | 101 | 5000 |
| 2 | Jane | 102 | 7000 |
| 3 | Alice | 101 | 8000 |
| 4 | Bob | 102 | 6000 |
| 5 | Carol | 103 | 5500 |

The query will return:

| DepartmentID | EmployeeCount |
|---|---|
| 101 | 2 |
| 102 | 2 |
| 103 | 1 |

This shows how many employees are present in each department.

---

## Q2. Retrieve all orders placed by customers who have placed more than 3 orders.

**Solution:**

```
SELECT o.OrderID, o.CustomerID, o.OrderDate
FROM Orders o
WHERE o.CustomerID IN (
  SELECT CustomerID
  FROM Orders
  GROUP BY CustomerID
  HAVING COUNT(OrderID) > 3
);
```

**Explanation:**

- **Subquery**: The subquery inside the `IN` clause selects `CustomerID` for customers who have placed more than 3 orders. It groups the orders by `CustomerID` and then uses `HAVING COUNT(OrderID) > 3` to filter only those customers who have placed more than 3 orders.
- **Main Query**: The main query retrieves `OrderID`, `CustomerID`, and `OrderDate` from the `Orders` table where the `CustomerID` matches any of the `CustomerID`s returned by the subquery (those customers who have placed more than 3 orders).

**Example:**

Consider the `Orders` table:

| OrderID | CustomerID | OrderDate |
|---|---|---|
| 1 | 101 | 2024-01-01 |
| 2 | 102 | 2024-01-02 |
| 3 | 101 | 2024-01-05 |
| 4 | 101 | 2024-01-07 |
| 5 | 103 | 2024-01-10 |
| 6 | 101 | 2024-01-12 |
| 7 | 102 | 2024-01-15 |

The subquery will select `CustomerID = 101` because this customer has placed more than 3 orders. The main query will then return all orders for customer `101`:

| OrderID | CustomerID | OrderDate |
|---|---|---|
| 1 | 101 | 2024-01-01 |
| 3 | 101 | 2024-01-05 |
| 4 | 101 | 2024-01-07 |
| 6 | 101 | 2024-01-12 |

This query retrieves all orders placed by customers who have placed more than 3 orders.

---

## Q3. Write a query to find employees who earn more than the average salary of their department.

**Solution:**

```
SELECT Name
FROM Employees
WHERE Salary > (
  SELECT AVG(Salary)
  FROM Employees
  WHERE DepartmentID = Employees.DepartmentID
);
```

**Explanation:**

- **Subquery**: The subquery calculates the average salary for each department by grouping the employees based on their `DepartmentID`. The `AVG(Salary)` function computes the average salary for the employees within the same department.
- **Main Query**: The main query retrieves the `Name` of the employees whose salary is greater than the average salary of their respective departments. The `WHERE` clause compares the `Salary` of each employee to the average salary for their department (calculated by the subquery).

**Example:**

Consider the `Employees` table:

| EmployeeID | Name | DepartmentID | Salary |
|---|---|---|---|
| 1 | John | 101 | 5000 |
| 2 | Jane | 102 | 7000 |
| 3 | Alice | 101 | 8000 |
| 4 | Bob | 102 | 6000 |
| 5 | Carol | 103 | 5500 |

1. **Subquery Calculation**:
   - For `DepartmentID = 101`, the average salary is `(5000 + 8000) / 2 = 6500`.
   - For `DepartmentID = 102`, the average salary is `(7000 + 6000) / 2 = 6500`.
   - For `DepartmentID = 103`, the average salary is `5500`.
2. **Main Query**:
   - Employees whose salary is greater than the average salary in their department:
     - For `DepartmentID = 101`, Alice (Salary = 8000) earns more than the average salary of 6500.

- For `DepartmentID = 102`, Jane (Salary = 7000) earns more than the average salary of 6500.

The query will return:

| Name |
| --- |
| Alice |
| Jane |

This query identifies employees who earn more than the average salary in their department.

---

## Summary of Intermediate SQL Scenarios

1. **Counting Employees in Each Department**: The `COUNT()` function with `GROUP BY` aggregates data by department and counts the number of employees in each department.
2. **Orders by Customers with More Than 3 Orders**: Using a subquery with the `HAVING` clause, you can find customers who have placed more than 3 orders and retrieve their order details.
3. **Employees Earning Above Average Salary in Their Department**: A subquery calculates the average salary for each department, and the outer query selects employees whose salary exceeds that average.

These intermediate-level scenarios help you handle more complex queries involving grouping, filtering with subqueries, and comparisons, and they are common topics in SQL interviews.

4o mini

---

## 3. Advanced Query Problems

Here are two advanced SQL problems that help you practice complex SQL queries involving window functions, ranking, and aggregation.

---

## Q1. Find the top 3 highest-paid employees in each department.

### Solution:

```
SELECT Name, Salary, DepartmentID
FROM (
  SELECT Name, Salary, DepartmentID,
         RANK() OVER (PARTITION BY DepartmentID ORDER BY Salary DESC) AS Rank
  FROM Employees
```

```
) AS RankedEmployees
WHERE Rank <= 3;
```

**Explanation:**

1. **RANK()**:
   - The `RANK()` function is a window function that assigns a unique rank to each row within a partition. In this case, it ranks employees within each department by their salary in descending order (highest salary first).
   - For example, if two employees have the same highest salary in a department, they will both receive the rank of `1`, and the next employee will receive rank `3` (skipping rank `2`).
2. **PARTITION BY DepartmentID**:
   - The `PARTITION BY` clause ensures that the ranking is done separately for each department. Without this, the ranking would be global across all employees.
3. **ORDER BY Salary DESC**:
   - This orders the employees by their salary in descending order within each department, so the highest-paid employees are ranked first.
4. **Outer Query**:
   - The outer query filters the employees, selecting only those whose `Rank` is less than or equal to `3`, i.e., the top 3 highest-paid employees in each department.

**Example:**

Consider the `Employees` table:

| EmployeeID | Name | DepartmentID | Salary |
|---|---|---|---|
| 1 | John | 101 | 8000 |
| 2 | Jane | 101 | 7500 |
| 3 | Alice | 101 | 7000 |
| 4 | Bob | 102 | 9000 |
| 5 | Carol | 102 | 8500 |
| 6 | Dave | 103 | 9500 |
| 7 | Eve | 103 | 10000 |

- **Step 1**: The `RANK()` function will assign a rank to each employee based on their salary in descending order, partitioned by their department.

| EmployeeID | Name | DepartmentID | Salary | Rank |
|---|---|---|---|---|
| 1 | John | 101 | 8000 | 1 |
| 2 | Jane | 101 | 7500 | 2 |
| 3 | Alice | 101 | 7000 | 3 |
| 4 | Bob | 102 | 9000 | 1 |
| 5 | Carol | 102 | 8500 | 2 |
| 6 | Dave | 103 | 9500 | 2 |
| 7 | Eve | 103 | 10000 | 1 |

- **Step 2**: The outer query filters the employees to only include those whose `Rank <= 3`. In this case, all employees in the sample table are ranked within the top 3 of their department, so the final result will include all.

  **Final Output**:

| Name | Salary | DepartmentID |
|---|---|---|
| John | 8000 | 101 |
| Jane | 7500 | 101 |
| Alice | 7000 | 101 |
| Bob | 9000 | 102 |
| Carol | 8500 | 102 |
| Dave | 9500 | 103 |
| Eve | 10000 | 103 |

This query returns the top 3 highest-paid employees in each department.

---

## Q2. Write a SQL query to get the most popular products based on order count.

**Solution:**

```
SELECT ProductID, COUNT(OrderID) AS OrderCount
```

```
FROM OrderDetails
GROUP BY ProductID
ORDER BY OrderCount DESC
LIMIT 5;
```

### Explanation:

1. **COUNT(OrderID)**:
   - The `COUNT()` function counts the number of `OrderID` entries for each `ProductID`, effectively counting how many times each product has been ordered.
2. **GROUP BY ProductID**:
   - The `GROUP BY` clause groups the data by `ProductID`. This allows the query to aggregate order counts for each product.
3. **ORDER BY OrderCount DESC**:
   - The `ORDER BY` clause sorts the products by the count of orders in descending order, so that the most popular products (those with the highest order count) appear first.
4. **LIMIT 5**:
   - The `LIMIT 5` clause restricts the result to the top 5 most ordered products.

### Example:

Consider the `OrderDetails` table:

| OrderID | ProductID | Quantity |
|---|---|---|
| 1 | A | 2 |
| 2 | B | 1 |
| 3 | A | 1 |
| 4 | C | 3 |
| 5 | A | 4 |
| 6 | B | 2 |
| 7 | A | 5 |
| 8 | C | 2 |

- **Step 1**: The `COUNT(OrderID)` will count how many times each product appears in the `OrderDetails` table:

| ProductID | OrderCount |
|---|---|
| A | 4 |

| ProductID | OrderCount |
| --- | --- |
| B | 2 |
| C | 2 |

- **Step 2**: The `ORDER BY OrderCount DESC` will sort these counts in descending order, showing the most ordered products first.
- **Step 3**: The `LIMIT 5` ensures that we only retrieve the top 5 most popular products. In this case, since there are only 3 products, the result will return all of them.

**Final Output**:

| ProductID | OrderCount |
| --- | --- |
| A | 4 |
| B | 2 |
| C | 2 |

This query returns the most popular products based on the number of orders.

---

## Summary of Advanced SQL Queries

1. **Top 3 Highest-Paid Employees in Each Department**:
   - The `RANK()` window function is used to rank employees within their department by salary, and then a filter is applied to get only the top 3 employees.
2. **Most Popular Products Based on Order Count**:
   - By using `COUNT()` and `GROUP BY`, you can count how many times each product appears in the orders. Sorting the result with `ORDER BY` and restricting it with `LIMIT` helps you find the most popular products.

These types of advanced SQL queries are frequently asked in interviews to assess a candidate's ability to work with complex aggregations, window functions, and subqueries.

---

## 4. Real-Life Case Studies

**Problem:**
You have an `Employees` table and a `Reviews` table. Each employee has multiple reviews, and you need to find the average review score for each employee.

**Solution:**

```
SELECT e.EmployeeID, e.Name, AVG(r.ReviewScore) AS AverageReviewScore
FROM Employees e
JOIN Reviews r ON e.EmployeeID = r.EmployeeID
GROUP BY e.EmployeeID, e.Name;
```

**Explanation:**

- **JOIN**: The `JOIN` clause is used to combine the `Employees` table and the `Reviews` table based on the `EmployeeID` column. This ensures that we get data about the employees and their associated reviews.
- **AVG(r.ReviewScore)**: The `AVG()` function is used to calculate the average review score for each employee from the `Reviews` table.
- **GROUP BY**: The `GROUP BY` clause groups the data by `EmployeeID` and `Name` (from the `Employees` table). This allows the aggregation function (`AVG()`) to calculate the average review score for each employee individually.

**Example Data:**

| EmployeeID | Name | ReviewScore |
|---|---|---|
| 1 | John | 4 |
| 1 | John | 5 |
| 2 | Alice | 3 |
| 2 | Alice | 4 |
| 3 | Bob | 5 |

- **Step 1**: The `JOIN` operation merges the `Employees` table with the `Reviews` table based on `EmployeeID`.
- **Step 2**: The `AVG(r.ReviewScore)` function calculates the average review score for each employee.
- **Step 3**: The `GROUP BY e.EmployeeID, e.Name` ensures that the result is grouped by each employee.

**Output:**

| EmployeeID | Name | AverageReviewScore |
|---|---|---|
| 1 | John | 4.5 |
| 2 | Alice | 3.5 |

| EmployeeID | Name | AverageReviewScore |
| --- | --- | --- |
| 3 | Bob | 5.0 |

This query returns the average review score for each employee based on their reviews in the Reviews table.

---

## Q2. Real-Life Scenario: E-commerce Website - Customer Purchase History

### Problem:

You have an Orders table, a Customers table, and a Products table. Retrieve a list of customers who have purchased a specific product more than once.

### Solution:

```
SELECT c.CustomerID, c.Name
FROM Customers c
JOIN Orders o ON c.CustomerID = o.CustomerID
JOIN OrderDetails od ON o.OrderID = od.OrderID
WHERE od.ProductID = 101
GROUP BY c.CustomerID, c.Name
HAVING COUNT(od.ProductID) > 1;
```

### Explanation:

- **JOIN**: The JOIN clause is used to combine the Customers, Orders, and OrderDetails tables based on the related IDs (CustomerID, OrderID, ProductID). This ensures we have the necessary information to analyze the products purchased by each customer.
- **WHERE od.ProductID = 101**: The WHERE clause filters the results to only include orders where the ProductID is 101 (the specific product we are interested in).
- **COUNT(od.ProductID)**: The COUNT() function counts how many times each customer has purchased product 101.
- **GROUP BY**: The GROUP BY clause groups the data by CustomerID and Name (from the Customers table), so we can aggregate the data at the customer level.
- **HAVING COUNT(od.ProductID) > 1**: The HAVING clause filters the results to include only those customers who have purchased product 101 more than once.

### Example Data:

| CustomerID | Name | OrderID | ProductID |
| --- | --- | --- | --- |
| 1 | John | 1001 | 101 |
| 1 | John | 1002 | 101 |

| CustomerID | Name | OrderID | ProductID |
|---|---|---|---|
| 2 | Alice | 1003 | 102 |
| 3 | Bob | 1004 | 101 |
| 3 | Bob | 1005 | 101 |
| 4 | Eve | 1006 | 103 |

- **Step 1**: The `JOIN` operation combines all three tables (`Customers`, `Orders`, and `OrderDetails`) based on their respective IDs.
- **Step 2**: The `WHERE` clause filters the results to include only the rows where `ProductID = 101` (the product of interest).
- **Step 3**: The `GROUP BY c.CustomerID, c.Name` groups the results by customer, allowing us to aggregate purchases for each customer.
- **Step 4**: The `HAVING COUNT(od.ProductID) > 1` ensures that only customers who have purchased product `101` more than once are selected.

**Output:**

| CustomerID | Name |
|---|---|
| 1 | John |
| 3 | Bob |

In this case, John and Bob are the customers who purchased product `101` more than once.

---

## Summary of SQL Query Approaches in Real-Life Scenarios

1. **Employee Performance Review System**:
   - **Scenario**: Calculate average review scores for employees.
   - **Solution**: Use `JOIN` to combine data, `AVG()` for aggregation, and `GROUP BY` to group by employee.
2. **E-commerce Website - Customer Purchase History**:
   - **Scenario**: Find customers who bought a specific product multiple times.
   - **Solution**: Use `JOIN` to combine multiple tables, `WHERE` for filtering specific products, and `HAVING` to filter customers based on purchase frequency.

These types of queries are common in business environments where analyzing customer behavior or employee performance is critical. By using SQL's aggregation, grouping, and filtering features, you can extract meaningful insights from large datasets effectively.

## 5. Behavioral Questions on SQL Practices

*Q1. How do you optimize a slow SQL query?*

**Answer:** To optimize a slow SQL query, consider the following strategies:

1. **Use Indexing:** Ensure that columns used in `JOIN`, `WHERE`, and `ORDER BY` clauses are indexed.
2. **Avoid SELECT *:** Select only the necessary columns rather than using `SELECT *`.
3. **Analyze Execution Plan:** Use the `EXPLAIN` statement to analyze the query execution plan and identify bottlenecks.
4. **Optimize Joins:** Make sure that joins are done on indexed columns, and use the appropriate join type (`INNER JOIN` vs. `LEFT JOIN`).
5. **Use LIMIT:** When applicable, use `LIMIT` to reduce the result set size.

*Q2. Can you explain normalization and denormalization? When would you use each?*

**Answer:**

- **Normalization** is the process of organizing data in a way that reduces redundancy and dependency. It typically involves breaking down large tables into smaller, related tables. This improves data integrity and minimizes duplication.
    - **Use case:** When you want to avoid data redundancy and ensure efficient updates.
- **Denormalization** is the process of combining tables or adding redundant data to improve query performance by reducing the need for complex joins.
    - **Use case:** When read performance is critical, such as in reporting systems or data warehouses.

*Q3. How do you handle large datasets in SQL?*

**Answer:** Handling large datasets in SQL involves several strategies:

1. **Batch Processing:** Break down large queries into smaller chunks.
2. **Use of Indexes:** Ensure proper indexing on large tables to improve query performance.
3. **Partitioning Tables:** Use table partitioning to divide large tables into smaller, manageable pieces.
4. **Optimize Joins:** When working with large datasets, minimize the number of joins and use appropriate types of joins.
5. **Consider Query Caching:** Use query caching to avoid reprocessing large datasets for frequently executed queries.

## Conclusion:

SQL interview questions are diverse and test both theoretical knowledge and practical problem-solving skills. By preparing for common SQL questions—ranging from basic queries to real-life case studies—you can demonstrate your understanding of SQL's power and versatility. Advanced topics like subqueries, joins, aggregation, and optimization are crucial for real-world applications, while behavioral questions assess your experience and approach to database management.

---

# CHAPTER-14

## SQL FOR REAL-WORLD APPLICATIONS

## SQL in Data Analysis

**Data analysis** involves examining and processing data to extract useful information. SQL is widely used for querying, aggregating, and analyzing data from relational databases.

*Example: Analyzing Sales Data*

Imagine you have a `Sales` table that stores data about products sold, including product IDs, sales amounts, dates, and regions. You need to calculate the total sales per region and the average sales per product.

```
SELECT Region, SUM(SalesAmount) AS TotalSales, AVG(SalesAmount) AS AvgSales
FROM Sales
GROUP BY Region, ProductID;
```

### Explanation:

- **SUM(SalesAmount)**: Aggregates the total sales amount for each region and product.
- **AVG(SalesAmount)**: Calculates the average sales amount per product.
- **GROUP BY Region, ProductID**: Groups the results by region and product, allowing us to see total and average sales for each combination.

### Real-World Use Case:

- **Data analysts** use SQL queries like the one above to explore data from sales, inventory, and customer behavior. This helps them uncover trends, such as which products perform best in specific regions or time periods.

---

## 2. SQL for Web Development

SQL is crucial in **web development**, especially for building dynamic websites that interact with databases. Web applications often need to fetch, insert, and update data stored in databases. SQL enables developers to manipulate this data efficiently.

*Example: User Authentication System*

In a web application, you often need to retrieve user credentials for authentication from the `Users` table.

```
SELECT UserID, Username, Password
FROM Users
```

```
WHERE Username = 'john_doe' AND Password = 'hashed_password';
```

**Explanation:**

- The query fetches a user's `UserID`, `Username`, and `Password` from the `Users` table based on the provided credentials.
- **WHERE** clause filters data based on the input username and password.

## Real-World Use Case:

- **Web developers** rely on SQL to create login systems for websites, e-commerce platforms, and applications. They also use SQL for managing other data, such as product catalogs, order details, and user preferences.

---

## 3. SQL in ETL Processes

**ETL (Extract, Transform, Load)** is a critical process in data warehousing where data is extracted from source systems, transformed into a usable format, and loaded into a target system (such as a database or data warehouse). SQL plays a central role in each of these steps.

*Example: Extracting and Transforming Data*

Imagine you need to extract data from a `Transactions` table, transform it (e.g., calculate the total transaction value), and load it into a new table for reporting.

```
-- Extract and Transform: Calculate total transaction value for each customer
SELECT CustomerID, SUM(TransactionAmount) AS TotalSpent
FROM Transactions
WHERE TransactionDate >= '2024-01-01'
GROUP BY CustomerID;
```

*Load Data into New Table:*

```
-- Insert the transformed data into a new table
INSERT INTO CustomerTransactionSummary (CustomerID, TotalSpent)
SELECT CustomerID, SUM(TransactionAmount)
FROM Transactions
WHERE TransactionDate >= '2024-01-01'
GROUP BY CustomerID;
```

**Explanation:**

- **Extract**: The first query retrieves the transaction data for each customer and sums up their spending.
- **Transform**: The data is aggregated (summed up) to compute the total amount spent by each customer.
- **Load**: The second query inserts the transformed data into a new table `CustomerTransactionSummary`.

## Real-World Use Case:

- **ETL tools** and databases often use SQL to clean, aggregate, and transfer large datasets. Companies use SQL in ETL pipelines to move data from operational systems into data warehouses, making it easier to generate reports and conduct analytics.

---

## 4. Case Studies: Real-World SQL Usage

*Case Study 1: Customer Segmentation in Marketing*

**Problem:**
A marketing team needs to segment customers based on their spending behavior to run targeted promotions.

**Solution:**

```
SELECT CustomerID,
       CASE
         WHEN TotalSpent > 1000 THEN 'High Spender'
         WHEN TotalSpent BETWEEN 500 AND 1000 THEN 'Medium Spender'
         ELSE 'Low Spender'
       END AS CustomerSegment
FROM CustomerTransactionSummary;
```

**Explanation:**

- **CASE**: This SQL `CASE` expression classifies customers based on their total spending. High spenders are those who have spent more than $1000, while medium and low spenders are those in between or below.

*Real-World Use Case:*

- **Marketing analysts** use SQL to categorize customers based on their behavior, allowing targeted campaigns for different customer segments. This increases marketing ROI and engagement.

---

## Case Study 2: E-commerce Inventory Management

**Problem:**
An e-commerce website needs to track products with low stock and notify the warehouse team.

**Solution:**

```
SELECT ProductID, ProductName, StockQuantity
FROM Products
WHERE StockQuantity < 10;
```

**Explanation:**

- This query retrieves products with a stock quantity of less than 10, which can then be flagged for restocking.

## Real-World Use Case:

- **E-commerce platforms** use SQL to monitor inventory levels and avoid stockouts, ensuring that products are always available for customers.

---

## 5. Integrating SQL with Programming Languages

SQL can be integrated with various programming languages (such as Python, Java, and PHP) to build more powerful applications. Here's an example of how SQL is integrated with Python.

*Example: Python and SQL Integration*

In Python, you can use libraries like `sqlite3` or `SQLAlchemy` to connect to a database and execute SQL queries.

```
import sqlite3

# Connect to the SQLite database
conn = sqlite3.connect('ecommerce.db')

# Create a cursor object
cursor = conn.cursor()

# Execute a SQL query
cursor.execute("SELECT ProductID, ProductName, Price FROM Products WHERE
Price > 100")

# Fetch and print results
products = cursor.fetchall()
for product in products:
    print(product)

# Close the connection
conn.close()
```

**Explanation:**

- This code connects to an SQLite database, runs a `SELECT` query to get product information, and prints the results.
- **cursor.execute()** runs the SQL query, and **fetchall()** retrieves the results.

## Real-World Use Case:

- **Web developers** and **data scientists** use SQL within programming languages to build interactive websites, applications, and data analysis tools. SQL helps integrate database operations into more complex systems, enabling dynamic content generation, analytics, and automation.

---

## Summary

SQL is a powerful tool for solving a wide range of problems in real-world applications. Whether you are analyzing data, developing web applications, managing ETL processes, or integrating SQL with programming languages, the ability to write efficient SQL queries is essential in many fields. By using SQL effectively, you can:

- **Analyze and visualize data** to drive business decisions.
- **Develop dynamic websites and applications** that interact with databases.
- **Transform and load data** as part of an ETL process.
- **Integrate SQL with programming languages** to create sophisticated systems.

SQL is integral to building scalable, data-driven solutions in various industries like e-commerce, healthcare, finance, and more.

# CHAPTER-15

## LAB EXERCISES FOR PRACTICAL LEARNING

### BEGINNER-LEVEL EXERCISES

### 1. Writing Simple SELECT Queries

**Objective:**
Learn to retrieve data from a table using `SELECT` statements.

*Exercise 1: Retrieve all records from the Employees table*

```
SELECT * FROM Employees;
```

**Explanation:**

- The `SELECT` statement is used to retrieve data from a table.
- The asterisk (`*`) is a wildcard that signifies selecting all columns from the table.
- In this case, the query retrieves **all records** (rows) and **all columns** from the `Employees` table.

Example Output (hypothetical):

| EmployeeID | Name | Department | Salary |
|---|---|---|---|
| 1 | John Doe | HR | 50000 |
| 2 | Jane Smith | IT | 60000 |
| 3 | Emily Johnson | Finance | 70000 |

*Exercise 2: Retrieve specific columns from the Employees table*

```
SELECT Name, Salary, DepartmentID FROM Employees;
```

**Explanation:**

- Instead of selecting all columns with the `*`, you can list specific columns after the `SELECT` keyword.
- In this example, the query retrieves only the `Name`, `Salary`, and `DepartmentID` columns from the `Employees` table.
- This allows you to focus on the relevant data.

Example Output (hypothetical):

| Name | Salary | DepartmentID |
|---|---|---|
| John Doe | 50000 | 1 |

| Name | Salary | DepartmentID |
|---|---|---|
| Jane Smith | 60000 | 2 |
| Emily Johnson | 70000 | 3 |

*Exercise 3: Filtering data with the WHERE clause*

```
SELECT * FROM Employees WHERE Salary > 50000;
```

### Explanation:

- The `WHERE` clause is used to filter data based on a specified condition.
- In this case, the condition is `Salary > 50000`, meaning only employees with a salary greater than 50,000 will be retrieved.
- The `*` symbol is used to select all columns, but the filter applies only to rows where the `Salary` is above 50,000.

Example Output (hypothetical):

| EmployeeID | Name | Department | Salary |
|---|---|---|---|
| 2 | Jane Smith | IT | 60000 |
| 3 | Emily Johnson | Finance | 70000 |

---

## 2. Creating and Modifying Tables

### Objective:

Learn how to create and modify tables using SQL commands like `CREATE`, `ALTER`, and `DROP`.

*Exercise 1: Create a new table called "Customers" with columns for customer ID, name, email, and phone number*

```
CREATE TABLE Customers (
    CustomerID INT PRIMARY KEY,
    Name VARCHAR(100),
    Email VARCHAR(100),
    PhoneNumber VARCHAR(15)
);
```

### Explanation:

- The `CREATE TABLE` statement is used to create a new table in the database.
- `CustomerID` is defined as the primary key (`PRIMARY KEY`), which ensures that the `CustomerID` is unique for each customer and cannot be `NULL`.
- `Name`, `Email`, and `PhoneNumber` are defined as `VARCHAR` data types with specific lengths.
    - `VARCHAR(100)` means the maximum length of the `Name` and `Email` is 100 characters.

- `PhoneNumber` can hold up to 15 characters, which is typically sufficient for phone numbers.

Example Output (hypothetical):

| CustomerID | Name | Email | PhoneNumber |
|---|---|---|---|
| 1 | John Doe | john@example.com | 1234567890 |
| 2 | Jane Smith | jane@example.com | 9876543210 |

*Exercise 2: Add a new column "DateOfBirth" to the Customers table*

```
ALTER TABLE Customers ADD DateOfBirth DATE;
```

## Explanation:

- The `ALTER TABLE` statement is used to modify an existing table's structure.
- The `ADD` clause adds a new column to the `Customers` table.
- `DateOfBirth` is defined as a `DATE` data type, which will store date values (e.g., `YYYY-MM-DD`).

Example Output (hypothetical):

| CustomerID | Name | Email | PhoneNumber | DateOfBirth |
|---|---|---|---|---|
| 1 | John Doe | john@example.com | 1234567890 | 1990-05-15 |
| 2 | Jane Smith | jane@example.com | 9876543210 | 1985-12-25 |

*Exercise 3: Drop a column from the Customers table*

```
ALTER TABLE Customers DROP COLUMN PhoneNumber;
```

## Explanation:

- The `ALTER TABLE` command with the `DROP COLUMN` clause removes a column from the table.
- In this case, the `PhoneNumber` column is being removed from the `Customers` table. Once the column is dropped, all data within that column will be deleted as well.

Example Output (hypothetical, after dropping the column):

| CustomerID | Name | Email | DateOfBirth |
|---|---|---|---|
| 1 | John Doe | john@example.com | 1990-05-15 |
| 2 | Jane Smith | jane@example.com | 1985-12-25 |

---

## Intermediate-Level Exercises

## 1. Complex Joins and Subqueries

### Objective:

Learn to join multiple tables and use subqueries to retrieve complex data.

*Exercise 1: Perform an INNER JOIN to retrieve a list of orders along with customer names*

```
SELECT o.OrderID, o.OrderDate, c.Name
FROM Orders o
JOIN Customers c ON o.CustomerID = c.CustomerID;
```

### Explanation:

- **INNER JOIN**: This join type returns only the rows where there is a match in both tables. In this case, it returns orders and their corresponding customers.
- `Orders o`: Refers to the `Orders` table with the alias `o`.
- `Customers c`: Refers to the `Customers` table with the alias `c`.
- `ON o.CustomerID = c.CustomerID`: The condition specifies that the `CustomerID` field from the `Orders` table should match the `CustomerID` field from the `Customers` table.
- This query will return a list of orders (OrderID, OrderDate) along with the corresponding customer name for each order.

### Example Output (hypothetical):

| OrderID | OrderDate | Name |
|---|---|---|
| 101 | 2024-12-01 | John Doe |
| 102 | 2024-12-05 | Jane Smith |
| 103 | 2024-12-10 | Emily Clark |

---

*Exercise 2: Use a subquery to find products that have been ordered more than 5 times*

```
SELECT ProductID, ProductName
FROM Products
WHERE ProductID IN (
    SELECT ProductID
    FROM OrderDetails
    GROUP BY ProductID
    HAVING COUNT(OrderID) > 5
);
```

## Explanation:

- **Subquery**: A subquery is a query within another query. In this case, the subquery is used to count the number of orders for each product.
- **Inner Query**:
  - `SELECT ProductID FROM OrderDetails`: Selects the `ProductID` from the `OrderDetails` table, which contains information about which products were ordered.
  - `GROUP BY ProductID`: Groups the result by `ProductID` so we can count how many times each product was ordered.
  - `HAVING COUNT(OrderID) > 5`: Filters the products, keeping only those that appear in more than 5 orders.
- **Outer Query**: Selects the `ProductID` and `ProductName` from the `Products` table, but only for the products whose `ProductID` appears in the result of the subquery.
- This query will return a list of products that have been ordered more than 5 times.

## Example Output (hypothetical):

| ProductID | ProductName |
|---|---|
| 101 | Wireless Mouse |
| 102 | Bluetooth Headset |
| 103 | Keyboard |

---

# 2. Data Manipulation Tasks

## Objective:

Learn how to manipulate data using `INSERT`, `UPDATE`, and `DELETE` statements.

```
Exercise 1: Insert a new record into the Products table
INSERT INTO Products (ProductID, ProductName, Price)
VALUES (101, 'Wireless Mouse', 29.99);
```

## Explanation:

- **INSERT INTO**: This command is used to add new rows of data into a table.
- `Products (ProductID, ProductName, Price)`: Specifies the table (`Products`) and the columns into which the data will be inserted.
- `VALUES (101, 'Wireless Mouse', 29.99)`: Specifies the values to insert into each of the columns. Here, a new product with `ProductID` 101, name "Wireless Mouse", and price 29.99 is being added to the `Products` table.

### Example Output (hypothetical, after the insertion):

| ProductID | ProductName | Price |
|---|---|---|
| 101 | Wireless Mouse | 29.99 |
| 102 | Bluetooth Headset | 49.99 |

---

*Exercise 2: Update the price of a product in the Products table*

```
UPDATE Products
SET Price = 25.99
WHERE ProductID = 101;
```

### Explanation:

- **UPDATE**: The `UPDATE` statement is used to modify existing records in a table.
- `Products`: Specifies the table that will be updated.
- `SET Price = 25.99`: The `SET` clause specifies which column(s) should be updated and what the new value should be. Here, the price of the product with `ProductID` 101 is being changed to 25.99.
- `WHERE ProductID = 101`: The `WHERE` clause filters the rows to update only the product with `ProductID` 101, ensuring other rows are not affected.

### Example Output (hypothetical, after the update):

| ProductID | ProductName | Price |
|---|---|---|
| 101 | Wireless Mouse | 25.99 |
| 102 | Bluetooth Headset | 49.99 |

---

*Exercise 3: Delete a product from the Products table*

```
DELETE FROM Products
WHERE ProductID = 101;
```

### Explanation:

- **DELETE**: The `DELETE` statement is used to remove rows from a table.
- `FROM Products`: Specifies the table from which the rows will be deleted.

- `WHERE ProductID = 101`: The `WHERE` clause ensures that only the product with `ProductID` 101 will be deleted. If this clause is omitted, all rows in the table would be deleted, so it's important to use it carefully.

**Example Output (hypothetical, after the deletion):**

| ProductID | ProductName | Price |
|---|---|---|
| 102 | Bluetooth Headset | 49.99 |

---

## Advanced-Level Exercises

Advanced-level exercises focus on more sophisticated aspects of SQL, such as query optimization, database design and normalization, and the creation of stored procedures. These topics are crucial for building efficient, scalable, and maintainable databases and applications. Let's explore these topics in detail:

---

## 1. Query Optimization Scenarios

**Objective:**
Learn how to optimize queries for better performance by analyzing execution plans, indexing strategies, and reducing query complexity.

*Exercise 1: Optimize a query with a missing index*

```
SELECT * FROM Employees WHERE DepartmentID = 10;
```

**Optimization Strategy:**

- **Problem**: In the given query, the `Employees` table is being queried for records where `DepartmentID = 10`. If there's no index on the `DepartmentID` column, the database engine will have to perform a **full table scan**. This means it will examine every row in the `Employees` table to check if the `DepartmentID` matches `10`, which is inefficient, especially for large tables.
- **Solution**: To improve the performance, we can create an index on the `DepartmentID` column. An **index** is a data structure that helps the database engine locate rows more quickly by keeping a sorted list of values in the indexed column.

```
CREATE INDEX idx_department_id ON Employees(DepartmentID);
```

**Explanation:**

- **CREATE INDEX**: The `CREATE INDEX` statement is used to create an index on the `DepartmentID` column in the `Employees` table.
- **How It Helps**: Once the index is created, the database engine can use the index to quickly find rows that match `DepartmentID = 10`, rather than scanning the entire table. This significantly speeds up the query execution time.

**Benefits of Indexing:**

- **Faster Data Retrieval**: Indexing speeds up queries by allowing faster data lookup.
- **Reduced Disk I/O**: Indexes reduce the amount of data the database engine needs to read, thus reducing disk I/O operations.
- **Efficiency**: Especially beneficial for large datasets where scanning the entire table would be time-consuming.

---

## 2. Designing and Normalizing a Database

**Objective:**
Learn database normalization principles to design a well-structured database that avoids redundancy and maintains data integrity.

*Exercise 1: Design a normalized database schema for a Library System*

Normalization involves organizing data in a way that reduces redundancy and dependency. There are several normal forms (1NF, 2NF, and 3NF) that help in achieving an optimized database design.

**Steps for Designing the Database:**

- **1st Normal Form (1NF)**: Ensures that the table only contains atomic (indivisible) values. This means each column should contain a single value (no lists or arrays).
- **2nd Normal Form (2NF)**: Ensures that all attributes in a table depend on the entire primary key. If the table has a composite primary key (i.e., more than one column), it eliminates partial dependency.
- **3rd Normal Form (3NF)**: Ensures that non-key attributes do not depend on other non-key attributes (transitive dependencies).

For a **Library System**, the schema can be designed as follows:

### 1. Books Table (1NF):

- BookID (Primary Key)
- Title
- Author

The `Books` table is in **1NF** because each attribute holds atomic values: a book ID, a title, and an author.

### 2. Members Table (1NF):

- MemberID (Primary Key)
- Name
- Email

The `Members` table also adheres to **1NF**, storing individual attributes for each member.

### 3. Borrows Table (1NF, 2NF, and 3NF):

- BorrowID (Primary Key)
- BookID (Foreign Key from Books)
- MemberID (Foreign Key from Members)
- BorrowDate

The `Borrows` table tracks which member has borrowed which book and the borrow date. This table is in **2NF** because:

- There is no partial dependency: All non-key attributes (BorrowDate) depend on the entire primary key (BorrowID).

This table is also in **3NF** because:

- There are no transitive dependencies: Non-key attributes do not depend on other non-key attributes.

### Explanation of Normalization:

- By designing this schema, we avoid data redundancy (e.g., repeating member information in the borrowing records) and ensure data integrity.
- If a member updates their contact details, we only need to update one record in the `Members` table, instead of updating multiple borrow records.

### Benefits of Normalization:

- **Reduces Redundancy**: Data is stored only once, minimizing duplication.
- **Improves Data Integrity**: Changes made in one place are automatically reflected everywhere, ensuring consistency.

- **Optimized Storage**: By eliminating unnecessary duplicate data, normalized databases make more efficient use of storage.

---

## 3. Writing and Testing Stored Procedures

**Objective:**
Learn how to write and execute stored procedures to automate repetitive tasks and encapsulate complex logic in the database.

*Exercise 1: Create a stored procedure to calculate the total sales for a specific product*

```
DELIMITER //
CREATE PROCEDURE GetTotalSales(IN ProductID INT)
BEGIN
    SELECT SUM(SalesAmount) AS TotalSales
    FROM Sales
    WHERE ProductID = ProductID;
END //
DELIMITER ;
```

**Explanation:**

- **Stored Procedure**: A stored procedure is a precompiled set of one or more SQL statements that can be executed on demand. Stored procedures are used to encapsulate repetitive tasks or complex logic, reducing the need for writing the same query multiple times.
- `CREATE PROCEDURE GetTotalSales(IN ProductID INT)`: This creates a stored procedure named `GetTotalSales` that takes `ProductID` as an input parameter.
- `SELECT SUM(SalesAmount) AS TotalSales`: Inside the procedure, this query calculates the total sales amount for the specified product (`ProductID`). The `SUM()` function adds up all the sales amounts for the product.
- `DELIMITER //`: In MySQL, `DELIMITER` is used to define the start and end of the stored procedure. The default delimiter is `;`, but it's changed temporarily to `//` to avoid conflicts with the semicolons used within the procedure.
- **Benefit**: The stored procedure simplifies repetitive tasks. For example, the same query can be executed multiple times for different products, saving time and avoiding errors.

*Exercise 2: Call the stored procedure to get sales for a product*

```
CALL GetTotalSales(101);
```

**Explanation:**

- **CALL Statement**: The `CALL` statement is used to invoke a stored procedure. In this case, `GetTotalSales(101)` is called, which calculates the total sales for the product with `ProductID` 101.

- **How It Works**: When the stored procedure is called, the input parameter (`ProductID = 101`) is passed, and the result is returned, showing the total sales for that product.

### Example Output (hypothetical):

| TotalSales |
| --- |
| 5000.00 |

www.ingramcontent.com/pod-product-compliance
Lightning Source LLC
LaVergne TN
LVHW081755050326
832903LV00027B/1957